PARENTING PASSAGES

David Veerman

PARENTING PASSAGES

TYNDALE HOUSE PUBLISHERS, INC.
Wheaton, Illinois

Library of Congress Cataloging-in-Publication Data

Veerman, David.
      Parenting passages / David R. Veerman
         p.   cm.
      Includes bibliographical references.
      ISBN 0-8423-5038-1
      1. Parenting—Religious aspects—Christianity. 2. Parent and child—Religious
aspects—Christianity. 3. Parent and teenager—Religious aspects—Christianity.
4. Grandparenting—Religious aspects—Christianity. 5. Grandparent and child—Religious
aspects—Christianity. I. Title.
HQ769.3.V44   1994
      248.8′45—dc20   94-26143

Printed in the United States of America

99   98   97   96   95   94
6   5   4   3   2   1

To Kara and Dana—
miracle babies,
terrific kids,
and maturing young women
who have made each passage a joy

CONTENTS

ACKNOWLEDGMENTS

*Special thanks to the following parents and
veterans of many of the passages:*

Patty and Tim Atkins
Myrllis and Chuck Aycock
Mitzie and Bruce Barton
Marcee and Nelson Bennett
Joan and Bob Biastock
Rhonda and Bob Childress
Joe Coggeshall
Becky and Jack Crabtree
Anne and Dick Davis
Diane and Ken Davis
Julie and Tom Essenburg
Kathe and Jim Galvin
Claudia and Lee Gerwin
Judy and Jim Green
Sandy and Kirby Hanawalt
Barb and Charlie Havens
Cheryl and Doug Knox
Susan and Larry Kreider
Sue and Chuck Lewis

Sally and Hollis Loan
Ruthie and Daryl Lucas
Dottye and Lew Luttrell
Polly and Jim McCauley
Barb and Courtney Miller
Cindy and John Pickerl
Lorna and Don Ray
Rachel Ringenberg
Holly and Bill Sanders
Ruth and Mark Senter
Judy and Bob Stromberg
Babs and Dave Swanson
Linda and Tom Taylor
Darian and Paul Veerman
Gail Veerman
Karen and Neal Voke
Carol and Jim Wilhoit
Sherrie and Neil Wilson
Carol and Art Wittmann

INTRODUCTION

I *tore* the cardboard, pulled the pieces out of the large box, and laid each one on the garage floor. Attached to a couple of long poles were plastic bags filled with screws, washers, nuts, and bolts. *Let's see, here are the swings . . . this is the top . . . and this must be the glider. This shouldn't be too tough to put together.*

But my confidence in my ability to assemble the swing set quickly disintegrated into futility and anger. Nothing seemed to fit.

Sensing my growing frustration by my frequent outbursts, Gail sweetly offered a suggestion: "Honey, why don't you follow the directions?"

I muttered under my breath something about minding her own business, then returned to the task. But as soon as she left the garage, I quickly searched through the pile of discarded cardboard until I found "Assembly Instructions."

Then I started over, slowly this time, reading and taking each printed step, one at a time. Soon the swing set was ready to be carried to the yard.

It's amazing what can happen when you follow the directions.

Everything seems to come with instructions these days: VCRs, microwaves, bicycles, lawn mowers, telephones, and toys. Most computers even have built-in tutorial programs to ease new users into the age of information.

Wouldn't it be great if babies came that way—with detailed instructions on how to "assemble" their lives?

> **Doctor:** *Congratulations, Mr. and Mrs. Veerman. You are the proud parents of a brand-new, state-of-the-art baby girl.*

> **Mr. Veerman:** *But now what do we do? We've never had a baby before!*

> **Doctor:** *Not to worry. Here's the Kara Veerman Owner's Manual. I know it's a bit large and intimidating, but everything you need to know about taking care of your daughter is in this book. Just follow the instructions, and you'll do just fine.*

> **Mr. Veerman:** *What a relief! Parenting should be a breeze.*

Of course it doesn't work that way. Children don't come with detailed directions or surefire formulas for ensuring that they grow and develop into positive kids and mature young adults. Instead, parents must greet each baby anew, as a fresh, unique, and complex creation of a loving God. There are no test models. Mom and Dad don't get the chance to practice with a prototype of the child ahead of time. They must adapt and respond to each situation as it comes.

The truth, of course, is that *all* parents are amateurs . . . even the "experts." Our babies aren't born with a manual in hand, God's instructions for raising *this* particular child. And even previous parenting experience with older siblings gives woefully inadequate preparation, for each child is unique.

Perhaps most frustrating is the crash of parenting idealism. Before a baby's birth, especially with planned pregnancies, Mom and Dad both imagine the precious new member of the family gradually maturing under their sensitive and strong spiritual guidance. They may admit to the possibility of a few bumps, but for the most part, they think the ride should be smooth. Then, when life's bumps turn into mountains and the potholes into canyons, Mom and Dad are blown away, totally surprised and unprepared.

I've been a parent for nearly two decades. While that's not long compared to many, I have gained much personal experience in the field. In addition, having been in youth ministry for nearly all of my adult life, I have had the opportunity to counsel, discuss, laugh, and cry with hundreds of parents in the course of my work. And I have spoken with scores of my parenting peers: coworkers, church members, neighbors. Through my experience and countless discussions, I have realized that most parents encounter a series of crisis points with their children over the years. At each of these points or milestones, parents are caught off guard—surprised and even shocked by the child's actions and their own feelings. In discussing a personal parenting crisis with fellow parents, I have often found that they were relieved to know they weren't alone in their struggles. Others have experienced many of the same conflicts, tensions, and feelings.

I have identified eleven of these times of crisis—*parenting passages.* Of course, not everyone has the same experiences or emotions at each passage; every child and every marriage is unique. And you may encounter milestones with your children that I don't discuss in this book. But most parents seem to have these eleven in common.

I call these times of crisis and emotion "passages" because they are movements of change varying in length and complexity. Every passage includes positive and negative moments, and each one presents challenges that must be navigated. These passages are not psychosocial developmental stages but are transition times in the life of a parent.

Each passage involves the developing relationship between parent and child and a critical time in the life of the parent. For example, when I was almost eighteen years of age, I couldn't understand why parents cried at high school graduation ceremonies. High school just wasn't that difficult—a person would have to *work* at not graduating, I surmised. But thirty years later, when my eldest daughter, Kara, graduated, I cried. And I was surprised by my emotion. My tears flowed from a mixture of feelings both happy and sad. It was a joyous occasion, but it was also a reminder that my little girl was growing up . . . and away.

You don't have to be surprised by these times of transition. Although this book is not an owner's manual with detailed instructions for every occasion or a guarantee for parenting success, *Parenting Passages* will help prepare you to meet the challenges of each critical stage of child rearing. As you read this book, I hope you will think, *Someone knows what I'm going through and feeling. Someone understands!*

Understanding the passages of parenting can help you and your spouse

- ◆ be prepared for each one, not shocked by them.
- ◆ understand your feelings.
- ◆ avoid the problems each passage poses.
- ◆ take advantage of the opportunities each one provides.
- ◆ be better parents.
- ◆ be able to help other parents as they meet each passage.

Much of this book will be autobiographical, but I have also included examples, vignettes, and personal testimonies from more than seventy other parents. My hope is that you will see yourself in these pages, identifying with the passages you've already encountered and preparing for those to come. In case you're new at this, let me tell you: Parenting can be quite an adventure. I hope you enjoy the trip.

Making the Big Decision

1

Joey and Sally
   sittin' in a tree
   K-I-S-S-I-N-G!
First comes love,
   Then comes marriage,
   Then comes Joey with the baby carriage!

Remember that children's rhyme? We used it to tease friends who might have been seen with a member of the *(ugh!)* opposite sex. At that time of life, we weren't even interested in love, much less marriage and having babies. But at least we had the order right: love . . . marriage . . . baby. Whether or not we ever thought consciously about having babies (or even knew how babies were had), we probably assumed that someday we would be parents.

As we grew and matured and became *very* aware of the opposite sex, becoming a parent *someday* became a live option. In fact, with raging adolescent hormones inflamed by movies, television, books, and magazines, we had to work at *not* getting involved sexually and *making babies*.

At least that was my experience.

To balance the influence of my sex-crazed culture, I had strong Christian parents, an evangelical church, and Youth for Christ. I remember speakers at church camp and YFC rallies urging young people to save themselves for marriage. Their impassioned pleas helped. I wasn't aware of much talk about parenting in those days (no seminars, films, or video series—remember, this was before the information age). But I knew what a good parent was—someone like Mom or Dad who was committed to Christ, to each other, and to the family. So even through the stormy high school dating games and sexual pressures, I assumed that someday I would be a father.

Gail and I married at the ripe old age of twenty-six. That seems so young now, but at the time, we thought we were well on our way to *old-maidhood.* We followed the advice of marriage books and counselors, and we decided to wait a few years before starting a family. We believed that we should get to know each other first before expanding our family circle and multiplying the relationships. During this time we remained confident that eventually, when *we* decided, Gail would get pregnant and we would have a baby. Just a year later, however, the gynecologist explained that Gail's medical history indicated she might have difficulty getting pregnant. He suggested we think seriously about trying to start a family right away.

We were shocked by the news because we had assumed that we would be able to plan and structure our lives just as others had done. But we decided to proceed and were excited about the prospect of becoming parents. We shared the news with close friends and joked about the fun we would have *trying*.

But nothing happened.

After months and months of timing, taking temperatures, and following folk remedies and other advice, we came up empty. Each month, the onset of menstruation became more of a letdown, signaling another twenty-eight-day defeat. After more than a year of fruitless attempts to conceive, we both had tests to determine the cause of infertility. I was given pills to increase my sperm count, and Gail was subjected to special medical procedures, some of them quite painful. But still the results were negative.

I had always assumed that I would *beget* sons and daughters after the King James Version biblical pattern, and coming from a large family, I had never considered anything else. But as the reality of our situation sank in, I began to doubt, grieve, and even despair. And I prayed a lot! I also began to open my eyes to a number of childless couples in my experience and several others who had become parents through adoption. I thought about other potential moms and dads, like us, who must have experienced (or were currently experiencing) the same agonizing feelings, wanting desperately to bear children but feeling barren and impotent.

I wish I could say that during this struggle God gave me peace and a total acceptance of this as a possible *good* (see Romans 8:28) in his perfect will, but I wasn't that spiritually mature. I did, however, turn to God more during this struggle, and my faith was stretched.

Suddenly, one morning at school, Gail experienced severe cramping and began to bleed. Later, the doctor explained that she had suffered a miscarriage. We accepted the news with mixed feelings. We hated to lose the baby (even after so short a pregnancy), but we were encouraged with the realization that pregnancy was possible! So with renewed hope, we continued our quest to become parents.

A long two years later, the doctor's test confirmed what we already had guessed and desperately hoped to be true— Gail was pregnant! Thrilled beyond words, we wanted to let everyone know the good news, especially our relatives and friends who had been praying for us for months and even years. But because of Gail's history, we decided to wait until we were sure that everything was all right. After five months had passed with no complications, we began to spread the word. Our families and friends rejoiced with us.

It was late morning—near lunch, I think—I can't remember the time, but I'll never forget the experience. I was working on a maze for Campus Life's annual Halloween extravaganza when word filtered back to me: "Your wife is here."

Climbing down from my ladder, I walked quickly to the front of the building, avoiding plywood, nails, tools, and paint. The school where Gail taught fifth grade was just a few blocks away, so I thought maybe she had come to give me a message or just to see how things were going. But then I saw her, framed by the front door, with the school principal standing at her side, and I knew something was wrong. With tears streaming down her cheeks, she walked over, put her arms around me, and sobbed, *"The baby's dead!"*

During the weeks that followed, we grieved our loss and questioned God repeatedly. I remember crying out at night, *"Don't you trust us, God? What's wrong with us?"* Confident that I would make a good father and Gail a good mother, I couldn't understand why God wouldn't allow us to have children. What made it even more difficult was knowing of high school girls who had become pregnant after messing around in the backseat of a car—no high-tech, sophisticated medical prescriptions or procedures. What was terrible news to those kids would have been thrilling to us. It wasn't fair. We were angry, hurt, and sad.

Eventually we worked through our grief and came to accept, although with a struggle, God's sovereignty in our lives. And we began to try again.

I learned much through our struggle to conceive and the

miscarriages. It certainly tested my faith and deepened my relationship with God. I won't pretend that I came to fully accept the possibility that I might not father a child of my own, but I was moving in that direction. In addition, the whole experience brought Gail and me closer together.

I also learned that pain is the rule in life, not the exception. During my midnight cries to God, I assumed that we were being singled out or punished, and so I thought, *Why me?* Of course, a youthful misconception about life is believing that painful events happen to a minority of people and always *the other guy.* In the following weeks, however, I learned that miscarriages and problems in pregnancies are quite common. Many women in our church—too numerous to count—confided to Gail that they had miscarried several times before having three or four beautiful children. God began to teach me through this very difficult experience that pain is part of being a finite human and living in a sinful world.

A few months later, we again received news that Gail was pregnant. And nearly nine months later, almost six years after our wedding day, Gail gave birth to tiny Kara Beth. We were thrilled to have a child and were surprised again, a few years later, with another beautiful daughter, Dana.

The loss of an unborn child requires a special kind of grieving, because there is that huge dollop of the unknown. What would that child have been like? Who would the little one have become? To the husband even more so than the wife, that little one is nothing more than a theory, a loss described without ever being seen or touched. Parents of unborn children add those other factors in as they work through their grief.

Frank Minirth, et al., Passages of Marriage (Nashville: Nelson, 1991), pp. 114–115.

THE FIRST PASSAGE

The first passage of parenting is getting pregnant. The decision to conceive and the subsequent events are the very beginning of the parenting experience. If life begins at conception, then so does parenting. In fact, bonding with the baby actually begins during the months of pregnancy, especially between mother and child. After all, she carries the weight and responsibility of the new life inside her, and she feels the baby move, kick, roll, and even hiccup.

But even if conception does not occur immediately, the *decision* to try embarks us on the journey. Thus, this parenting passage signals the first crash of idealism for many couples who face the harsh reality that they may be childless. And reality hits even harder when parents-to-be suffer miscarriage or a stillbirth—all those dreams, hopes, and plans are dashed in one terrible moment.

Couples who experience such difficulties and losses can find great help and support if they will seek it. For example, Bill and Holly Sanders went through a multitude of tests to discover the cause of their inability to conceive. Bill shares, "Finally we realized that we probably would never be fortunate enough to biologically father and mother our own child. We started going to infertility groups to find out how other people were coping."

For Kirby and Sandy Hanawalt, infertility was not only a matter of broken dreams, but also a threat to Sandy's health: *Sandy was diagnosed with a tumor in her brain. The doctors gave two options: they could surgically remove it, or we could try to have a baby! (Pregnancy and breast-feeding cause this type of tumor to shrink and often disappear.) This condition, however, also can reduce the possibility of pregnancy.*

During a year of trying without results, I found myself pulling further and further from Sandy. To handle the pain of our failure, I retreated into myself. Why could "everyone else" get pregnant so easy? Was there something wrong with me? Before long, I found myself not wanting children because I could not handle any more failure.

Our relationship began to deteriorate quickly. I would find any reason to not have sex with Sandy; I would even start arguments just to get her to back off from pressuring me. I felt angry at myself for not succeeding, angry at Sandy for having this physical condition, and, finally, angry at God for not taking this condition away.

Long after I had given up, the doctor called to say that we finally had succeeded. I wish I could say that I was overjoyed, but I had worked so hard to control my emotions that they now seemed dead to this exciting news. During the next four months, our relationship continued to be strained. Sandy was excited, but I could not feel her joy.

Hope in our relationship came when we decided to see someone for help. Instead of allowing us to hide our anger, disappointment, and frustration with God and each other, the therapist forced us to explore and verbalize our pain. By talking and sharing difficult feelings, we were able to renew our commitment to each other and to God.

God was gracious enough to provide us with a child. But it comforts me to know that when God seemed so far away, he allowed me to voice my anger and fear. He really does care!

In contrast to Kirby and Sandy, some couples have no trouble getting pregnant the first time, but then everything changes. Barb Miller explains: *We stopped using birth control and became pregnant right away. When Justin was about ten months old, Courtney and I thought we were ready to have a second child, and we assumed that it would happen as quickly as the first time. But month after month I did not become pregnant. I became obsessed with the idea—it was all I could think about. I became depressed, and my self-image plummeted. I felt as though God was angry with me and was punishing me. It took many years of God working in me— through friends, pastors, counselors, and prayer—for me to accept my infertility. A part of this acceptance was realizing that this was God's plan for my family and that God is the One who brings life.*

Of course, not all couples have a difficult time conceiving and bearing children. For some it happens just like in the books and their dreams.

When we decided to have our children, I succeeded in getting pregnant virtually as soon as we started trying. This was a great blessing, especially since Jim and I had waited until we were older to get married. We were thrilled to avoid a long delay. But we realized that we had to be very careful in sharing our joy about this, for fear of hurting the feelings of many others who had not been as fortunate. Many of our friends had struggled with difficulties in trying to get pregnant. Unfortunately, the end result was that we didn't feel free to share our joy with anybody.

Kathe Galvin

PLANNED FAMILIES

With a wealth of sophisticated medical counsel and procedures available to most American couples today, many take great pains to plan their pregnancies. But even when everything seems to work just as the doctor ordered, some problems usually arise. For example, in many cases, the first pregnancy and delivery are so painful and potentially life threatening for both mother and child that Mom and Dad wonder if they should risk having other children. For others, the first child seems easy compared to the next one. And, of course, there are an unlimited number of variations: multiple births, breech deliveries, birth defects, and other unplanned complications.

For my brother Paul and his wife, Darian, getting pregnant wasn't a problem, nor were they too concerned about the financial implications of a new baby—until seven months into the pregnancy when they learned they were going to have twins. That was an unexpected complication, but it turned into an unexpected joy.

No matter how much a couple plans and no matter how sophisticated our technology becomes, anything can happen! We still have to trust God for the outcome.

SURPRISES

Many couples are surprised with the positive results of the pregnancy test: the newlyweds who were going to wait until after getting established in their marriage and jobs, the career couple planning to wait until they were financially secure, the parents of two who weren't sure they wanted more.

Linda Taylor shares her experience when she discovered that she was pregnant with their third child: *What were these tangled emotions I was feeling? While I couldn't get a handle on the emotions, several facts (or at least what seemed to be facts) were clear:*

1. My husband, Tom, and I had planned on only two children. Now another baby was on the way, which would mean we'd had three babies in thirty-three months. I wasn't even sure that was physically possible.

2. If it was physically possible, I was sure it wouldn't be financially possible. How would we pay for another hospital bill? We were still paying off the bill from the last baby.

3. My body would never be the same. Three babies in less than three years. I would be nothing more than a blob.

4. I wouldn't have the energy to give to three children so young.

5. Our youngest child had just started walking and eating on his own. I really didn't want to start all over again with a new baby.

6. People were going to think my husband and I were, well . . . I was embarrassed to think about what they might think.

As with Linda and Tom, there is often shock at the news: some are immediately overjoyed, while others are dismayed. A good friend of mine and his wife had decided not to have children, so the doctor's report turned their world upside down. Throughout the pregnancy, this friend struggled with his attitude. After all, a baby would revolutionize their lives! But everything changed during delivery when he instantly fell in love with his newborn daughter (more about this passage in the next chapter).

After the initial shock, reality sets in, when plans and decisions must be made. Hopefully the couple soon comes to accept and welcome the impending arrival of this new family member.

Linda Taylor continues with her story: *When I got my perspective back, I could truly thank God for another baby, and I could eagerly look forward to the child's coming.*

*Sure, we had our embarrassing moments—"You're pregnant **again**?" asked well-meaning friends. Strangers gave me second glances as I walked through the grocery store with two kids in the cart and one in my bulging belly.*

But then he arrived. That tiny little miracle, completely

dependent on us for nurture and protection. He came and we love him as dearly as we love our other two children who, without hesitation, welcomed him into the family with too-hard hugs and wet kisses.

Art and Carol Wittmann had gotten married during college. After a stint in the military, Art had returned to college. He remembers clearly when he got the call: *Carol was at work when she got the results of her pregnancy test. I was in class when she called, so I was given the message to call her as soon as possible. When I called her back, she told me that the results were positive. We were thrilled. Although we really hadn't planned on starting when we did, it worked out fine.*

In another situation, both the mother and father were stunned with their fourth pregnancy bulletin. Although not what they had planned, soon the whole family became excited about the baby on the way. When the mother began to experience cramping and bleeding, the doctor predicted an imminent miscarriage. The family mourned their impending loss, accepted God's will, and began to make plans *without* the baby. But then the bleeding stopped and the doctor changed his prognosis, so the family had to readjust their thinking and planning again. Although they didn't enjoy the emotional roller-coaster ride, today the parents are thrilled with their fourth child, a daughter who has brought them much joy over the years.

ADOPTIONS

Many adoptive parents have been unable to have children of their own, so they have gone through the grieving process—denial, depression, bargaining, sadness, acceptance, and resolution—and have accepted, with tears, their situation. Still wanting to be parents, they have chosen to adopt orphans or unwanted babies borne and birthed by others. The adoptive process can be long, expensive, and emotionally draining. And it is not always easy. Waiting for news from adoption agencies can be excruciating and can last for years. And often hopes can be raised, only to be dashed by government red tape or a birth mother's change of heart.

Emily is three years older than the twins, and all of them are adopted. One of the twins, Brandon, was praying at the dinner table and thanking God for this and that. Then he said, "And thanks for letting Emily help Mom and Dad pick us out."

The beautiful thing about adoption is that you can let your child know that you chose her. Of all the children in the world, you chose her to come and live with you. You chose to love her. You chose to honor her in your home. You chose her to be part of your family forever.

Bill Sanders

Doug Knox says: *Seven years were filled with anxiety, first with trying to get pregnant and then actively seeking the opportunity for God to bless us with a child through adoption. Our answer finally came when a nurse introduced us to our newborn daughter and told us that our first official task would be to change her diaper.*

As we held Sara for the very first time, she smiled! And we cried tears of joy. I felt God's smile on us that day and sensed that this was his good plan. Just twenty-two months later, God blessed us again with the adoption of our son, Stephen.

Doug and Cheryl counsel couples who want to adopt: *Don't give up. God's plan is unfolding, and your joy will be multiplied by your struggles.*

Barb Miller explains that after she and Courtney accepted the fact that they would not be able to conceive again, they were able to look at other options for having a larger family: *A friend asked if we had ever thought about adoption. God opened our eyes, and we began investigating it. Eventually we traveled to Romania to adopt our daughter. One thing I will say about adoption—the husband and wife need to be in full agreement concerning this major decision because they will need each other for emotional support.*

When Bill and Holly Sanders realized they would be unable to have children of their own, they put their name on the adoption list of the Roman Catholic agency in town (they were nominally Roman Catholic at the time). Three years into the wait, they became born-again Christians and, two years after that, decided to change churches. When they informed the adoption agency that they were attending the Baptist church, the agency advised them to wait. Most of the girls who came to them wanted a Catholic home for the child. Bill reports: *Deep in my heart, I knew God was in control, and I told the agency representative, "God will reveal himself through our adoption. I just know it. Since the beginning of time, he has known who our first baby will be."*

About a year later, we received a call. They said, "We've got your baby!" When we saw her, we fell instantly in love with this five-month-old beauty from heaven. When I asked the woman from the agency why they chose us, she answered, "That's the best part of the story. The birth mother came in here a month after the baby was born. We were almost ready to adopt her into another family, the one next in line and higher on the list than you, but the birth mother said to wait. Then she came in and explained that she had become born again, just like both of you, and had joined a Baptist church. She said she wanted her baby in a Baptist home." Then the agency representative looked at me and said, "You were the only Baptists on our list!"

Holly and I returned home and knelt beside our couch and wept. We praised God and prayed for that birth mom—God's guiding led her to us. We have since told our daughter, Emily, that one day she will meet her birth mom, in heaven if not before.

Adoption is a wonderful option.

HOW TO RESPOND

No matter how prepared we think we are for each parenting passage, usually we will be surprised by the struggle and our feelings. The greatest shock for many couples is here, at the beginning, at conception and pregnancy. Youthful idealism crashes headlong into reality. As I described earlier, I was stunned by the difficulty of not being able to conceive and the possibility of not being able to father children. Others are hit abruptly with impending parenthood as they confront a surprise pregnancy. And even in planned pregnancies when things go just as the books and doctors describe, marriage strains and parenting anxieties can blindside expectant parents. But you don't have to be devastated. Taking a few practical steps can help you safely navigate through this passage.

I can't remember being aware, except in a dim way, that my in-laws had lost two children, both the result of early childhood complications. That is until we were expecting our first. We sensed but really didn't understand the mixture of anticipation and fear that my wife's parents expressed during our pregnancy. We didn't appreciate until later that they were fearing for us, for what we might be facing. I can vividly remember being struck by their reserved excitement when I called during the night with the news that our son had been born. They were trying to rejoice with us but were reliving their own past loss and grief at the same time. And they couldn't help but remember that birth doesn't make life certain, only obvious. The arrival of each child changes the whole world. That would be a cliché if it were not sometimes so painfully true.

Neil Wilson

---

1. Look Ahead

Although no one can be perfectly prepared for the emotions of pregnancy and birth, couples can get ready by understanding the process. It will be helpful for women to know about morning sickness, bloated feelings, back pain, and other possible discomforts and inconveniences of being pregnant.

Husbands should learn as much as they can about the process and realize their responsibility during these critical nine months. No man will ever be able to truly understand what it feels like to be pregnant and to give birth, but husbands should try. Then they will be able to empathize and feel more like partners in the process and will be able to support their wives emotionally. Husbands should also be prepared to adjust their schedules to help their wives cope, shouldering much of the burden of housework, caring for the other children, shopping, and so forth when necessary. Parenting should be a team effort that begins *now* and continues after the birth.

Engaged couples find it nearly impossible to imagine that they might have marital stresses and strains, no matter how much they are counseled or how many problems they know of in other marriages. I've counseled many such couples. They look at me, smile, say they understand, and then refer to their deep love for each other. I know, of course, that their love will be severely tested during the first couple of years of their marriage, but they sincerely believe that they will be exceptions—their marriage will be different. Some may say that it's not worth trying to counsel idealistic young people in matters of the heart, but even with their romantic ideal-ism, I believe that these couples are better off hearing warnings of potential struggles and that these problems are normal than not knowing about them at all.

The same is true for potential parents. Here also idealism is high and denial great, especially for Christians. Most are confident of their ability to raise a perfect little child in a positive Christian atmosphere. Yet each passage of parenting tempers that idealism with reality. So you should be ready and, as much as you can, prepare for possible emotional shocks along the way.

2. Build Support

A person's support system should include their family: spouse, parents, siblings, and grandparents. But others can also provide support: neighbors, coworkers, and especially close Christian friends. Even in planned pregnancies where everything seems to be going smoothly, couples should ask friends to pray for them—for safety, good health, and wis-dom. Galatians 6:2 commands: "Carry each other's bur-dens, and in this way you will fulfill the law of Christ" (NIV). Clearly, believers have a responsibility to care for each other. Sometimes we think, however, that we need to carry the weight of this burden by ourselves, so we never confide in others and reveal our questions, fears, hopes, and dreams. In so doing, we cheat ourselves out of fellowship, concern, counsel, and care, and we deny others the opportunity to participate with us in the miracle of birth.

Several years ago, a woman in our church shared with

Gail her and her husband's deep desire to have children. They had been unable to conceive and had been trying to adopt for a few years. This woman asked if Gail and I would pray for them about this situation, as others were doing. We considered it a privilege to be involved with them that way. And we rejoiced with them when they finally were able to adopt. What a wonderful answer to prayer!

Other great sources of support are parenting and Lamaze classes, and other groups organized to train or support prospective or expectant parents. Usually these are offered through hospitals, YMCAs and other community organizations, and churches. You could even start one in your church. Besides the advice and counsel from the leaders, you can learn much through conversation with others in the group.

Don't try to go it alone—seek to build a support network.

3. Seek Help

Some people are too proud to admit that they might have a problem. This seems to be a trait of the male of the species, especially when it comes to conception. Often the husband will assume that it must be the woman's fault, but there are many possible causes. If getting pregnant is difficult, get professional help—consult a physician.

Other problems arise where help should be sought. For example, a couple can feel overwhelmed by the financial stresses—they can't imagine stretching their income to feed another family member. They should ask for help from someone who can analyze their financial situation and guide them toward solutions. Another couple may be struggling with fear about parenting or coping with depression after a miscarriage. They should seek a counselor who can help them through this difficult time in their lives.

Again, this is where the church can play a crucial role. Most churches have resources, financial and personal, to help struggling members. Our church isn't large, but we have a professional counselor who is a member, and his services are available. Like many counselors, he uses a sliding scale for his fees, depending on the person's ability to pay. We also have two pediatricians in our congregation. In addition, our deacons have a fund to help with special needs, and they supervise an active mercy ministries team.

Usually help can be found if you look for it.

THE CHALLENGE

Many of us have unrealistic expectations or preconceived notions about parenthood when we first begin to consider having children. But as Daryl Lucas recalls, the plunge into parenting may prove to be an important step toward our own maturity: *I thought getting married was a real adult thing to do. We left home. We moved away. We paid our own bills. Don't mess with me, I'm twenty-three. My memories of our first pregnancy will remain with me for a long time, however, precisely because that's when I **really** grew up. For nearly three years of marriage, life had consisted of a simple equation: 1 + 1 = 2. Ruthie and I enjoyed each other. We made decisions together. Our time was our time. **Our lives affected only us.***

We suffered from the desire to have kids just as much as most young couples do. And we put it off, just as many do, to build our own relationship first. But starting a family had a very strong appeal. It was the natural thing to do. A rite of passage. "Only big people have babies." Our desire to have children grew each year.

*The day The Test came back positive, **wham**—it hit me. This was it! Life would **never** be the same again. From now on, no matter what happened, my life would **forever** be changed. Even if the pregnancy ended in a miscarriage, we would carry the loss and disappointment with us. If the pregnancy went well and the child was born, we would suddenly have a little person to take care of, to provide for. We'd have to spend money on this person for years and years and years. And even after this child left home, our lives would be affected by him, by his absence, by the memories we had of him growing up. **Life would never, ever be the same!***

That's the day I grew up. If I had any doubts that getting married was an adult move, this put them all aside.

Whether you enter the first passage of parenting through pregnancy or adoption, you are in for a wonderful, exciting, life-changing, sometimes terrifying adventure. Life will never be the same again—and that's just the way God planned it.

LET'S THINK ABOUT IT

With each succeeding chapter, an increasing number of readers will not have experienced that specific passage. But since this is the first, most of you have probably made it through this passage. Thus, as you read the *warnings, oppor-*

tunities, lessons, and *resources,* think of how you can use this information, combined with your experience, to counsel other potential parents.

Warnings

- *Hold on to your plans loosely—God may have other ideas* (see Proverbs 16:9 and James 4:13-15). Go ahead and make your plans, even for when you hope to have children, but be ready to adjust them and to move in a new direction.
- *Don't believe the notion that bad things only happen to others.* If you do, you may be devastated when they happen to you. Instead, be prepared for the pain by living with gratitude to God for each day. Also realize that God will be with you in the middle of your trials, to comfort and lead you (see Matthew 6:33-34, John 16:33, and 1 Corinthians 10:13).
- *Don't try to struggle alone.* Share your concerns with friends and loved ones and seek help.
- *Be sensitive to couples who may have had difficulty conceiving,* and offer to pray for them when they share their struggle with you.

Opportunities

- *Use your struggles* to stretch your faith and increase your dependence on God (see Romans 8:28).
- *Become a person of prayer,* committing your future and your new child to God.
- *Support others* who are trying to conceive or adopt,

through encouragement, prayer, and friendship (see
Galatians 6:2 and Philippians 2:1-4).
- *Use your experiences to help others* who may be in pain.

Lessons

- *Pain is the rule, not the exception of life.* Many couples
  experience great difficulty getting pregnant, and many
  women experience complications in pregnancy, including miscarriages.
- *God's way may not be easy, but it is best.* Our response
  should be to trust and obey.
- *Life truly is a gift from God.* We should choose life, value
  life, and celebrate life, and we should take our parenting
  responsibilities very seriously. Children are entrusted by
  God to our care.

Resources

- *Bethany Christian Services* is a Christian organization
  devoted to helping children and families. In addition to
  offering counseling and other family services, they help
  couples adopt children. For more information, write to
  901 Eastern Avenue, NE, Grand Rapids, MI 49503-
  1295, or call 616-459-6273.
- *Evangelical Child and Family Agency* provides a broad
  range of services to individuals, couples, and children,
  including personal counseling, training, foster care, do-
  mestic and international adoption, special-needs adoption, and pre- and postadoption counseling. They can

be contacted by writing 1530 N. Main St., Wheaton, IL 60187, or by calling 708-653-6400.

◆ Angela Elwell Hunt, *Loving Someone Else's Child* (Wheaton, Ill.: Tyndale House, 1992). This book covers the spectrum of those who need to love *other people's* children, including stepparents, grandparents, foster parents, guardians, adoptive parents, and others. It contains insightful counsel and practical help for all kinds of parents and a wide variety of parenting situations.

Seeing the
Miracle

———

2

You feel warm and comfortable in your quiet, soft, dark home. Regularly fed, you have no worries and no complaints. In fact, you even have room to tumble and swim in your watery environment. And the regular background sound of a heartbeat gives you assurance and security. You've known no other way to live, and life is good!

All at once you feel the pressure, a tightening, holding you motionless as the walls of your home begin to pull in around you. Panic! Fear! A few seconds later, the walls relax and the pressure subsides. But soon it happens again and again with greater frequency. Eventually the walls push almost continually, with only brief moments of respite, and you feel yourself being forced downward and squeezed. The pressure becomes intense until you are pushed out and away from your home, down and through a narrow channel. Everything seems wrong and out of control—you know it's the end.

Suddenly strong hands grip your head and pull you away from the pressure and the constricting tunnel, out of your now terrifying home to freedom. But the light is blinding and the air cold. Sputtering for breath, you gulp as your lungs begin to function. And you cry from frustration and pain—and for help! Tender hands rub your tiny arms, legs, and body, wrap you in a blanket, and hand you to loving arms that pull you close.

Welcome to the world—you've been born!

That's an imaginative (if not scientific) look at birth from the baby's perspective. From Mom and Dad's perspective, this second passage of parenting is nothing short of a miracle! Even the most cynical or blasé person can feel overwhelmed by the wonder of a new life entering the world. Recently, I was listening to a sports talk show on a local radio station. One of the regular guests, a former NFL player and tough-as-nails all-pro, called in to the show from the hospital. He was at his wife's side, having just observed the birth of his first child. Although not a religious person, he gushed about the *miracle* he had witnessed.

~~~~~~

I was among the first wave of dads to invade the delivery room. We stormed the fortress and then didn't know what to do with ourselves when we arrived.

Here's a warning: *Don't try to experience someone else's feelings.* I talked to several other recent dads before my own turn under the bright lights, and I was told that I would have an unforgettable, transcendent experience. I would marvel at the miracle, be touched to the core of my being. I began to anticipate what I was about to feel almost as much as I looked forward to the birth of our child. Instead, I ended up being a kind of helpless double spectator. I watched my son being born while I watched myself and tried to identify and analyze what I was feeling. The wave of emotions never swept over me. I think I was too busy keeping track of my feelings to actually let them happen. Every birth is unique. Don't miss your experience watching for feelings that someone else may have had.

Neil Wilson

~~~~~~

I have heard that new father's comment repeated again and again. Ken Davis says that he had set up a video recorder and other cameras in the delivery room so that he could record the birth of his first child. He thought he was totally prepared for the moment—it was *show time.* But Ken was so overcome with emotion that he forgot to use the cameras. He could only watch and weep.

I was not allowed in the delivery room for Kara's birth, but three and a half years later I had that privilege when Dana was born. I will always remember the thrill of seeing the crown of her head pushing through, followed by the rest of her precious body. And I will never forget our Christian doctor's profound and glorious announcement as he held Dana up for us to see: "Praise the Lord! It's a girl! And her first breath is from God!" Seconds later, he carefully handed her to Gail. What a fantastic opportunity and privilege! There she was, a miniature human being—and part of us, one made from two. We wept and prayed and marveled at Dana's perfectly formed features, knowing that there was no more beautiful baby in the world and that, together, we had participated in a holy event.

Both pregnancies and births gave me a deeper appreciation and love for Gail, my wife and the mother of our children. She endured such pain, especially in delivery, yet she bore each child with patience and love. It's a good thing that men don't give birth—I'm too much of a wimp to go through what mothers endure. But I thank God for Gail, her courage, and her resilience.

***

Kathe and I have a friend who is a real joker—the kind of guy who has a new joke every day. When we told him that we were starting Lamaze classes, Terry told me, "Jim, take my advice. Don't—I repeat—

don't crack any jokes in Lamaze class. You'll really get in big trouble." (He said this with a straight face.) Well, it was pretty difficult for me to hold back when we started the class. We had a rather humorless group, but I couldn't resist one comment on the second or third evening. I thought it was really funny. But to my genuine surprise, nobody laughed. At that moment, I decided that Terry had given me crucial advice that was important to pass on to other men.

Jim Galvin

As with other parenting experiences, the milestone of birth will have different expressions for different people. But in every case, bearing a child is a breathtaking miracle.

My brother Paul reflects: *The birth of the twins gave me an understanding of the pain of birth, and it was a life-changing experience to realize that those were **my** babies. Immediately, I was emotionally attached to them, and I was overwhelmed with the reality that "I'm a father!"*

Carol Wittmann explains that she gave birth to her oldest daughter, Heather, before husbands were allowed in the delivery room. In addition, she was given an anesthetic that put her completely out. She says: *The biggest surprise for me was waking up after giving birth and being told, "Congratulations, it's a girl." All of a sudden I was a mother, but I felt the same as before. The feelings associated with motherhood came later.*

Carol's husband, Art, remembers driving to the hospital and realizing the implications of having a third "somebody" in their family: *I thought, "From now on we won't be able to come and go as we please. We'll have to take Heather with us—along with a diaper bag and all sorts of supplies." It was a reality check. Before the birth of the first child, most parents don't think of all the little stuff involved in having a baby and rearing a child.*

Barb Miller reflects: *Justin's birth went quite easy, and the Lamaze techniques helped so that I did not require any pain medication. I pushed hard a few times and there he was! And he was just perfect! I was overcome with joy and praise to God. And I was so excited and exhilarated that I couldn't go to sleep that night. I kept offering prayers of thanksgiving to God for this precious little guy that God had entrusted to us.*

To help prepare myself for the blessed event, I exercised all through pregnancy, even though it looked silly. Did you ever see a bunch of pregnant women running around a gym? We looked like a volleyball game where every player had the ball.

I also took a natural-childbirth course. It was terrific. They used to put all of us pregnant mommies into gym suits and lay us down on the gym floor to do our exercises. We looked like a relief map of the Rocky Mountains. They explained everything that would happen during labor. At the end, they even showed a movie of a woman giving birth to her

baby. I enjoyed that part the most. But for some reason, they threw me out of class. Maybe it was because I asked them to run the movie backward.
"Come on nurse," I shouted, "now let's see the baby
disappear."

*Joan Rivers, Having a Baby Can Be a Scream (New York:
Avon, 1974), p. 35.*

In addition to birth, this second passage includes the
weeks and months that follow, when the parents bring the
baby home and adjust to having a new member of the
family. Especially with the firstborn, Mom and Dad confront a variety of new feelings, many of them quite surpris-
ing.

THE JOURNEY

Gail's and my struggle to conceive and to carry a baby to
term was only part of the story leading to Kara's grand
entrance into the world. We also had nearly nine months of
difficult pregnancy.

Right up front I must confess that, as a man, I will never
fully understand the miracle of birth. Certainly I was there
at the time of conception, but no matter how hard I tried to
be involved during gestation, I could only be an appreciative
spectator, observer, witness, cheerleader, and coach. Gail,
however, was deeply and personally involved. Every day she
was reminded that another person was living inside her.
Often those reminders brought joy as she felt the baby move

or thought of our soon-to-be-born child. But they also brought sickness, pain, discomfort, fatigue, eroding self-esteem, and other frustrating side effects.

In all pregnancies, the growing baby pushes the mother's internal organs, causing a variety of problems. In addition, all pregnant women are supposed to watch what they put their bodies through and what they eat and drink—after all, they're eating for two. And let's not forget the matter of physical size; as the baby grows, so does Mother—outward. After seven months, most pregnant women feel slow, fat, and ugly. Many a husband has regretted his attempts at humor about his wife's size.

Gail's pregnancy with Kara was not easy. When she began to swell, the doctor put her on a salt-free diet. At one point, her face seemed to have swollen to about twice its size—couples from our Lamaze class didn't recognize her at the reunion. In addition to the headaches and nausea, Gail experienced increasing back pain as the months passed. And because of having miscarried previously, we had to be very careful about what we did and where we traveled. Sex was out of the question for the entire pregnancy, and we were told to stay home for the holidays. Gail wasn't allowed to lift anything heavy or to do much housework, so I carried the grocery bags and vacuumed the house. Obviously, our routine changed drastically.

One morning, late in the pregnancy, Gail began to experience severe abdominal pain, so I rushed her to the hospital, fearful and unnerved. The cause was not cramps or contractions but a gall-bladder attack, a relatively common side effect of having one's insides pushed around, we were told.

Despite all these physical and emotional annoyances, Gail's medical checkups continued to be positive. In fact, at about the eighth month, the doctor reported that the baby was growing and should be a *big baby.*

A couple of weeks before the due date, a group of women from our church held a baby shower for Gail. When I picked her up afterward, she complained of back pain. Thinking it was just another pregnancy annoyance, we headed home. We assumed that Gail had been on her feet too long and just needed to lie down and rest. But the pain continued and seemed to intensify at regular intervals. At 11 P.M. we called Gail's doctor. He told us to note the time between the incidents of intense back pain and to call him back if the intervals got down to five minutes. We called him again at 1 A.M. "It may just be a false alarm," he said, "but you may be in labor." So we quickly packed and took our well-rehearsed drive to the hospital.

THE BIRTH

At the hospital, doctors confirmed that Gail was, in fact, in labor . . . back labor. Back labor occurs when the baby lies face up instead of face down. This causes the back of the baby's skull to hit the mother's tailbone, resulting in almost constant pain and making it difficult to distinguish between contractions. It is one of the most painful types of labor.

I joined Gail in the labor room, coached her in shallow breathing and focusing, timed the contractions, and waited.

A nurse who took Gail's blood pressure seemed alarmed and asked Gail questions about her medical history. Then she called Gail's doctor, who was delivering a baby at another hospital. Next came a steady stream of doctors, nurses, interns, students, and tourists (so it seemed). Every time they examined her, she would have a contraction. (Later we learned that Gail had a special condition that brought all this attention and curiosity.) Finally, at about 10 A.M., Gail's doctor arrived, checked her out, and rushed her into the delivery room. A nurse ushered me to another room, where I was informed that Gail had acute toxemia, so I couldn't accompany her.

I didn't know what the nurse meant, but I joined other expectant fathers in the waiting room. After not too long— but what seemed like an eternity—the doctor emerged, called me in, and congratulated me on the birth of my new daughter.

Kara was twenty-one inches long but weighed only five pounds. Gail is not a big woman, but I'm six feet, three inches and weigh 210 pounds—we wondered how we could have produced such a small baby. Later I learned that acute toxemia is a serious condition involving poison in the bloodstream. During the last two weeks, Kara had been losing weight. If the pregnancy had gone two more weeks (to the due date), we could have lost her. In fact, both Gail and Kara could have died during delivery. All of this reinforced our belief that we had a *miracle baby*, and we thanked God for his sovereign care and personal love for us.

In the recovery area, we praised God for our little bundle

of miracle, enfolded in love and wrapped in our arms. Other than a short bout with jaundice and having to be warmed to normal body temperature, Kara did well during her first few days in the world. Because she was so small, the nurses nicknamed her Peanut. Five days later, we were able to take her home (at four pounds, thirteen ounces).

THE ORDEAL

Of course we were thrilled to have our new family member. I was fascinated by Kara's tiny features, especially her perfect fingers with minuscule nails. The crib seemed huge when we laid her in it. We had spent years preparing for this moment. The room was ready, and we thought we were too. But our idyllic picture of a peaceful, cooing baby was shattered when we discovered that Kara had a severe case of colic. Her stomach was perpetually upset, especially while she was being fed, so she cried loud and often.

Most newborns bring sleepless nights for parents, but our situation was extreme, with numerous up-and-downs during the wee hours. The next day I would drag into the office, held alert by numerous cups of coffee. Many times Gail would take Kara downstairs to the family room so that I would be far from the cries and could get some sleep. Feeding Kara could take as long as two or three hours rather than the normal twenty minutes, leaving Gail physically and emotionally exhausted. This condition lasted three months.

Even between feedings, at night Kara would awaken, fuss,

and have to be settled down. Gail and I took turns getting up with her.

A typical two o'clock incident would go something like this:

1. Kara would cry and need attention.

2. Although it was my turn to rock Kara back to sleep, I would pretend to be asleep and hope that Gail would take pity on me and get up instead.

3. Guilt and my sense of duty would get to me, and I would go across the hall to Kara's bedroom, pick her up, hold her on my shoulder, and sit in the rocking chair.

4. I would try a four-movement technique to get Kara back to sleep: patting her on the back, bouncing her gently, rocking the chair, and singing or humming softly to her.

5. Eventually, Kara would stop crying, calm down, and go to sleep on my shoulder. However, the next trick was getting her back in the crib without waking her up.

6. I would stop rocking but continue bouncing, patting, and humming.

7. I would stand up and stop bouncing but continue patting and humming.

8. I would walk to the edge of the crib and stop humming but continue patting.

9. I would place her in the crib while lightly patting her back, pull up the blanket, and then tiptoe out of the room and back across the hall to our bedroom.

10. I would quietly slip into bed, get comfortable, and try to go back to sleep.

11. *WAAAAAH!* Kara would cry, and the process would be repeated.

This would continue until finally Kara would stay asleep for three or four more hours. The morning came very quickly.

THE THOUGHTS AND FEELINGS

I took all this space to describe what we went through with Kara because of what I learned through this experience, this passage.

First, *I began to understand child abuse.* Don't misunderstand me—abusing a child is never justified, and I didn't come close to hurting mine. But there were times when I was so tired, frustrated, and defeated that I found myself becoming angry with Kara. Remember, this was our miracle child, the one for whom we had prayed day and night. Yet I was angry with her. Sometimes only the love of Christ and the restraint of the Holy Spirit kept my temper in check. And I thought that it must take an extremely mature and self-controlled person to keep a grip *without* an awareness of God's love and support. Here, after all, is a crying child who has *intruded* into their lives. With reason clouded by lack of sleep and emotions running high, the results might easily be disastrous.

It wasn't Kara's fault that her stomach was often upset and that her only way of responding to her hurts was with tears and screams. She wasn't deliberately keeping me from a good night's sleep—she was acting like a baby. But I found myself angry. Frustration and even anger are common feelings—and yet they can catch us by surprise.

Bruce and Mitzie Barton already had a daughter and two sons when, after much prayer, they decided to have one more child. Mitzie confesses: *I really wanted another girl and was so sure that God would give me my heart's desire. So when Erik was born, I was shocked. Later I realized that I was mad at God, and my anger was affecting my feelings for my son—it wasn't his fault. I had to work through these emotions, confess my anger to God, and trust that his way was best.*

Claudia Gerwin went back to work, thirty hours a week, when Abby was just a month or so old. Claudia's mother lives with her and Lee, so she took care of the baby when Claudia was at the office. Claudia's routine often left her exhausted. She explains: *Abby was the kind of baby who slept best when held by someone—her mother. We tried putting her down in the crib, slightly awake, but she would cry and scream until she was picked up again. If we put her down after she fell asleep, she would awaken instantly and start yelling. She had us well trained!*

One evening, when Abby was about two months old, I decided that it was time for her to learn to sleep in her crib. I was so tired that I could hardly see straight. What I really needed to do was to go to bed and turn over her care to my husband or Mom, but I was determined to teach her this important lesson. I nursed her, cuddled her, and, when she was mellow, put her down. She started screaming. I comforted her, following all the rules about checking on her every five minutes, not picking her up, singing to her, calming her, but firmly telling her that she needed to sleep in her crib. After about two hours of this, we were both in tears—she in her crib and me sitting on the floor in the hallway outside her room.

Reflecting on these experiences and her feelings, Claudia says: *I certainly don't condone child abuse in any form. After this experience, however, I think I can understand a bit better the utter helplessness and frustration such parents must feel when they are exhausted and without resources before they lose control and commit such a terrible act as beating their child.*

Sometimes our feelings cloud our reason and determine our actions.

My second discovery as I endured sleepless nights and struggled to care for our precious child is that *I was overwhelmed by a tremendous sense of gratitude to my parents* for what *they* had endured with me. Certainly my mother must have suffered during her nine months of carrying me inside her. Certainly she had suffered in labor, bringing me into the world. Certainly Mom and Dad had suffered trying to get me to sleep at night and trying to pay the bills for their new family member. Certainly they had questioned their parenting skills, had sought helpful counsel, and had prayed much over the years. Yet as the recipient of that care and concern, I had been virtually oblivious to their sacrifices and work on my behalf, taking it all for granted. Mom and Dad had never mentioned what they had done for me as though I owed them something. But I did. And I didn't realize it until 3 A.M. as I changed Kara's diapers, dried her tears, and rocked her to sleep for the third time that night.

I also thought about how that experience would be repeated by my children. Kara and Dana will never truly understand our love and what we went through for each of them until they have children of their own. (Even if I tell them or they read this, they won't *feel* it.) The waiting, praying, crying; the difficult pregnancies and dangerous births; the sleepless nights—all were investments in their lives and symbols of our love.

Third, *I began to get a glimpse of what unselfish love is all about.* When I lost sleep and sat rocking, bouncing, patting, and humming to Kara, I did it out of love, expecting nothing in return. The next day, Kara couldn't get up and say, "Thanks, Dad. I know I had a rough night, and I really appreciate what you did for me!" Instead, she would repeat the difficult routine.

For the first time in my life, I found myself giving unselfishly, without strings attached, knowing that I would get nothing in return . . . at least not for many years. I loved Kara deeply because of who she was and not for anything she could do for me.

About the time Matt learned to talk, he had a series of ear infections. The doctor at the clinic informed me that my son had a wax plug that he was going to have to soften by gently squirting warm water into the ear and then draining it out. "What I'm about to do will probably cause some pain for your boy. Can you hold him while I work?" Matt realized something was up when I changed the way I was holding him in order to immobilize his arms. He began to cry as soon as the doctor touched his ear. I held my struggling son during the procedure as he called out, over and over, "Daddy, it hurts, it hurts!" I felt so utterly helpless. I wanted to hit the doctor. My instincts to protect my child were being violated, and they didn't appreciate it one bit.

That moment comes to mind every time I seek to grasp what it meant for God the Father to stand by while his Son was nailed to a cross in order to bring about our healing.

Neil Wilson

In those early morning hours, I thought of God's love for me, and I gained fresh insight into the verse I had learned as a child: "For God so loved the world that he gave his one and only Son" (John 3:16, NIV). God gave and gave and gave. And what could I possibly do to repay Christ for his love and sacrifice for me? Nothing. While I was a sinner, deserving only condemnation and punishment, Christ died for me (see Romans 5:7-8). I can only give him my life.

And I thought of how I ought to reflect God's love to

others, loving them as he has loved me (see 1 John 4:10-11). Too often, however, my love and good deeds have conditions on them. I expect people to respond, to give something back—at least a thank-you. In fact, if they don't, my feelings get hurt and I feel slighted or used. As I cared for Kara, God began to teach me about love.

Fourth, *I learned how to pray for my child,* my miracle baby. During those sleepless nights, I spent a lot of time talking with God about Kara and thinking about what she would become. Would she be beautiful? Intelligent? Spiritual? Charming? Witty? Athletic? A world changer? I tried to be like Hannah, who gave her child, Samuel, back to God (1 Samuel 1:22-28). I wanted to trust God fully for her future. This has been a constant struggle over the years—I give the girls to God but then keep trying to take them back.

I also prayed for myself and my new responsibilities as a parent, asking God for strength and wisdom. I talked to God about my fears. Investing myself in Kara heightened my anxiety about possibly losing her. And I wondered what kind of parent I would be. Would I know how to encourage, love, guide, and discipline Kara? Would I be a good example of a godly parent? Although I had counseled many parents on how to rear their teenagers, at that moment I felt as though I didn't have a clue about parenting. I felt like a little kid looking under the hood of a car, knowing where the engine was but little else. I began to realize that I would need help and counsel and that I would have to rely totally on God.

Doug Knox had a similar experience when he discovered

the potential joy in night feedings: *One of the benefits of bottle feeding is that Dad can help. Responding to a cry at 2:30 in the morning and rescuing that tiny, helpless child from hunger is an enormously satisfying experience. I remember sitting and rocking for an hour past the time the tummy was filled and the eyes closed, thanking God for this precious life and praying for protection and guidance.*

These feelings don't necessarily change with future children. When Dana was born, I was overwhelmed once again by the miracle of birth (especially since I could be an eyewitness), the potential of *this* child, and the awesome task of being a parent.

I remember my son's first sneeze. He was newly born and only hours into this world. My wife, accompanied by a nurse, was holding him and proudly showing our son to his grandmothers. There was oohing and aahing and all of the delightful sounds that come from admiring grandparents. Then it happened. My son sneezed.

I couldn't believe it. No one else seemed to have noticed a thing. Then he did it again. I looked from one face to another in utter amazement as the doting continued without missing a beat. I was concerned and with good reason. After all, no one else in the room had been sneezing, but my newborn son had just done so, twice. As a brand-new father, I felt it was my responsibility to point out to the at-

45

tending nurse that my son was in need of medical attention because he's just sneezed.

I'll never forget the look she gave me. I knew instantly that I had just said the first foolish thing of my career as a parent. She assured me that children will do this from time to time and that sneezing was not at all abnormal. At that point I began to realize that this parenting thing was going to be trickier than I'd first thought.

Bruce Howard, You Can't Spank a Kid in a Snowsuit (Wheaton, Ill.: Tyndale House, 1994), p. 57.

HOW TO RESPOND

Again, during this passage, the idealism of being a parent meets reality. Usually we imagine our babies peacefully sleeping through the night and then innocently cooing and happily playing during the day. The reality is that most babies keep their parents up at night. Someone has suggested that this is caused by night nurses in the hospital who want to play with the babies. When the babies go home, they have the routine reversed, continuing to play at night and sleep during the day. Whatever the cause, even without colic many babies deprive their mothers and fathers of precious sleep.

Daryl Lucas says: *In **The Jungle Book**, Bagheera the panther discovers a baby in the middle of the jungle. He narrates: "If I had known how deeply I was to become involved, I would have obeyed my first instinct and walked away." That's what* *went through my mind at 3:00 this morning as I changed Jacob's diaper. Since our first (of three) was born nearly five years ago, I've averaged between four and five hours of sleep a night. Lately it's been solidly at four. I'm not exaggerating.*

*That's my biggest memory, my biggest impression of the preschool years: constant, unrelenting tiredness. When I get a little extra sleep, I feel no better. I'm **always** exhausted. And when I get brief snatches of "free" time, my list of "essential things you gotta do" is so long that even **it** gets neglected. The sink is piled high with dishes. Or there's no underwear.*

I laugh when people ask me if I "have time for . . ."

*The needs of my kids at this age are incredibly unrelenting. They **always** need something—I'm always feeding, changing, helping, soothing, comforting, bathing, dressing, undressing, answering, playing with, explaining to, etc. Yes, as they get older they gain skills and can do things on their own—and that has helped as far as it can—but it also seems that each new skill has only replaced one set of needs with a new one.*

My sister, Barbara Havens, is a nurse and midwife in Chicago. She tells me that one thing most new mothers, even those who are very poor, have in common is their glorified idea of motherhood. Many even think it will be fun to have a newborn at home. Barb tries to warn them of the work involved and the emotional and physical energy needed for the task, that birth is just the first step of about eighteen years together. She will see many of these mothers a few months later and ask how they're doing and how they enjoy being moms. The response is usually a tired "It's all right." The previous enthusiasm has disappeared.

In light of what giving birth and caring for babies actually requires, you can:

1. Work Together

Parenting should be a team effort and not the responsibility of just one parent. In many cases, however, the mother gets stuck with all the dirty work. A new grandparent friend of mine was bragging about her son-in-law to me recently. She was thrilled (and amazed) that he took such a hands-on, personal interest in caring for the baby. "When Clarice messed her diaper, John just picked her up, took her into the bedroom, and changed her!" Grandma was surprised because that action would have been unusual for men of her generation.

A mother at church told me that she almost went crazy with one of her children—he was such a handful. She cared for her son alone during the day because her husband had to work. But when he came home, she willingly allowed him to take over.

I don't want to minimize the joys of parenting. It's thrilling to watch the first step, hear the first word, see the smiles, hear the laughs, jiggle, cuddle, and play. But parenting can be intense. One mother of two toddlers and a baby explained that she yearned for an adult conversation. All day she had only heard simple sentences and demands for her attention.

Those of us whose children have moved beyond this stage should be sensitive to those who are in the middle of it. We can offer to baby-sit and give a harried couple a night out or take meals to a new mom and dad.

Church should also be a place where parents of babies and toddlers can find help. Our church believes strongly in the covenant community and that babies of Christian parents are children of the covenant, part of the family of faith. Thus we take seriously our commitment to working together as a church to care for those little ones. In fact, members will stand and pledge to do just that for a specific child. This translates into taking turns at working in the nursery and at providing child care for all services and events. I was caught short at an elders' meeting when a fellow elder with two small children reminded the rest of us of the need for child care. How quickly I had forgotten about those years when our freedom was limited and we had to spend a fortune on baby-sitters.

Remember that parenting is a team effort—help your spouse take care of the baby.

2. Be There

Many studies have shown that the first few months of life are critical for children. They need love and attention, to be cared for and held. Without loving touch, babies develop deep-seated feelings of insecurity and fear. Yet every day we hear of babies left alone or in the care of small children while the parents run errands or go to work.

In this age of self-centeredness and greed, parents can be tempted to avoid the inconvenience and annoyance of an infant. Although they could live without the second income, they quickly hire baby-sitters so they can rush back to work.

I believe this can be a shortsighted and even selfish

mistake. Spend time with your baby. Even though every moment won't be pleasant, value each one. Realize that the infant is totally dependent on you. The child won't be able to return your love for many years or appreciate fully what you have done until reacing adulthood, but your investment in your child's life will pay dividends. The baby, even at this early age, is learning to trust.

> All a newborn baby really needs is food, warmth, and love, pretty much like a hamster, only with fewer signs of intelligence.
>
> *Dave Barry*

Realize also that each child is unique with their own personality and temperament. Thus you will have to adjust your parenting efforts to meet the special needs of each child. Darian Veerman explains: *By having twins, I noticed right away how different they were—even as babies. Each one entered the world with his and her own personality.* From Darian's experience as a nurse, she has observed and spoken with many new parents. She adds: *Before they have the first child, many parents decide exactly what they will do. They have a program for discipline and everything. But it doesn't work that easily. As kids grow, parents have to adjust to different person-alities. Paul and I noticed Crista's sensitivity right away. All we had to do was let her know that we were displeased with her action and she would cry. We needed to be much more firm with Erik. Actually, Crista would cry when we disciplined Erik.*

Some parents just try to endure the first few years of a child's life and hope they can make it through as quickly and easily as possible. But this is a crucial time in your baby's life. Thank God for the opportunity to develop trust, love, and security as you spend time with your child. Don't ignore your responsibility or assign it to a stranger.

3. Be Patient

Although time seems to creep by during late-night feedings and long days nursing a sick child back to health, soon those days will pass. Eventually morning comes, as do the second, third, fourth, and fifth birthdays. And before you know it, you will be looking back on those days nostalgically and wondering where the time went.

During one Christmas vacation, we got out all our old super-8 movies and watched them together, the four of us. The movies were silent, so even when Kara or Dana was crying, we couldn't hear it. And in every frame they looked so cute and cuddly. More than once I had to choke back the tears as I watched them sleeping, playing, or being bathed, fed, and held. They grew up so fast!

James 1:2-4 reminds us, "Dear brothers, is your life full of difficulties and temptations? Then be happy, for when the way is rough, your patience has a chance to grow. So let it grow, and don't try to squirm out of your problems. For when your patience is finally in full bloom, then you will be ready for anything, strong in character, full and complete"

(TLB). Be patient during the difficulties in this passage. Your child will grow through it—and so will you.

4. Get Help

Earlier I described my feelings as I tried to calm Kara in the wee hours of the morning. I said that I began to understand child abuse because I was feeling anger toward my precious little girl.

For whatever reason, some parents aren't able to restrain themselves, and they take out their anger and frustration on their children. One of the greatest tragedies of our time is violence directed toward children. Daily we hear of parents who have seriously injured or even killed their babies or toddlers.

Babies are always more trouble that you thought—and more wonderful!

Charles Osgood, CBS Morning News

If you find that you can't control yourself or that you are moving dangerously close to the edge of your emotions and may explode at your child, get help. Go to your pastor, a close Christian friend, or a professional counselor. Whatever you do, don't take it out on your baby. Remember, it's not their fault. Your child is a priceless gift from our loving God and must be handled with care. Get help.

Experiencing the birth of a child and welcoming that child into your family will change your life. Filled with the whole range of emotions, this is perhaps the most profound passage of parenting. As you bring your baby home, *work together* with your spouse in caring for them, *be there* during this very important time of life, *be patient* as you suffer through sleepless nights and other inconveniences, and, if you need to do so, *get help.*

LET'S THINK ABOUT IT

Warnings

- *Don't be too idealistic about having a child.* While bringing much joy, babies also bring stress and work.
- *Don't assume that you can continue your regular schedule and family routine.* A new baby will change your life!
- *Be prepared to lose sleep and to learn new skills* such as how to burp a baby, how to change a diaper, how to feed a baby strained spinach and squashed peas, and how to live with the smell of spit-up on your shoulder.

Opportunities

- *Learn to look for God's miracles* beyond birth in everyday life.
- *Learn to depend on God* for your child's well-being and future and for your parenting skills.
- *Spend precious hours and days with your child,* bonding together.
- *Thank your parents for what they have done for you over the years.*

Lessons

- *God is intimately involved in the birth of every child* (see Psalm 139:1-13, 16).
- *God's love is giving, unselfish, and always with us* (see Romans 8:38-39).
- *Being a parent is a God-given privilege and an awesome responsibility* (see Deuteronomy 11:19-21; Ephesians 6:4).

Resources

- *Christian Parenting Today.* This bimonthly magazine is filled with helpful advice for parents of children of all ages. Special articles and regular columns are insightful and practical. For subscription information, write to P.O. Box 3850, Sisters, OR 97759, or call 503-549-8261.
- Greg Johnson and Mike Yorkey, *Faithful Parents, Faithful Kids* (Wheaton, Ill.: Tyndale House, 1994). Described as containing "a strategy for passing the baton of faith," this book is packed with hands-on, practical steps that you can take with your children to help them grow into young men and women, and eventually adults, who love and serve God.
- Nancy L. Swihart and Ken R. Canfield, *Beside Every Great Dad* (Wheaton, Ill.: Tyndale House, 1993). Although written primarily to mothers and focused specifically on fathering, this book emphasizes parents working as a team. This book is filled with biblical and practical help for all parents.

Introducing
Your Child
to the World

~~~~~~~~~~~~~~~

3

Beep, *beep!* Without slowing, Roadrunner speeds round
the hairpin turn on the edge of the mountain. In hot pursuit
on his ACME jet-powered bicycle, Wile E. Coyote fails to
make the turn, flies off the road, pauses for a second or two
in midair, and crashes to the canyon floor several hundred
feet below. Climbing slowly out of the coyote-shaped crater,
bruised and battered Wile E. shakes his fist at Roadrunner,

who has paused to watch from the canyon ledge. Then, *Beep, beep!* and the pesky bird is gone again.

In the next scene, Wile E. is putting the finishing touches on a huge, coyote-like robot. With its long legs, the giant radio-controlled machine is able to cover thirty yards in a single stride. Seeing Roadrunner in the distance, Wile E. sets the control to Seek and Destroy and points the robot toward his feathered prey. With Wile E.'s metal accomplice closing quickly, it looks as though the speedy bird will be caught. But Roadrunner circles around and behind, thus tricking the robot into thinking that Wile E. is the one to seek and destroy. The coyote-robot does just that, of course, flattening the hapless coyote with one step of his enormous, steel foot. Roadrunner *beep, beeps* and speeds out of sight as Wile E. peels himself off the ground, defeated again.

I used to enjoy watching Roadrunner cartoons, and before that *Mighty Mouse, Tom and Jerry,* and others. I thought nothing of the violence, lifestyles, and values they portrayed. But that changed with young children in my house. Suddenly I found myself becoming supersensitive to what Kara or Dana might see or hear. Even innocuous shows like *The Smurfs* would make me cringe sometimes.

Knowing each child's innocence and naiveté and wanting them to stay that way, I had a tremendous desire to protect my babies from all the terrible influences in the world. Often we would play together in the family room in front of the TV, or the girls would sit with us as we watched our favorite television shows. It was frustrating when questionable scenes would pop up and angry words would be spoken. Even during a positive, family-oriented show, offensive advertisements would intrude.

That was nearly sixteen years ago. Today, broadcast conditions have deteriorated so much that nearly every show contains patently offensive material. Some cable channels offer a steady stream of near pornography, radio DJs often use sexually explicit segues, pop musicians sing and rap violent and profane lyrics, and even news programs feature ratings-grabbing stories of sex and violence. Profanity that would have been censored when my children were young is commonly broadcast these days. The movie industry has continued to produce corrosive and depraved films, and their rating system has become a joke. The only way you can know if a movie is acceptable for your kids to see is to see it yourself.

These broadcasts invade our lives through a wide variety of instruments—radios, tape and CD players, portable TVs, headsets, video games, and computers—and in almost every environment.

Perhaps the biggest change during the past decade or so has been the avalanche of videos. Most families have VCRs attached to their TV sets. As with the television, stereo, and computer, this electronic appliance can be used for good or evil. Christian companies have produced many outstanding videos that entertain while teaching positive, Christian values. But Hollywood produces more of the other kind. In fact, every week new video releases are announced and made available through the mail, outlets in every strip mall, and even grocery stores.

The video revolution has spawned music videos, popularized through MTV (Music Television) and featured on other cable channels and in network programming. The influence of this form of entertainment cannot be overstated. When I began working with high school students in the late sixties and early seventies, kids were into popular music in a big way, as they still are today. Some of the rock groups promoted drug use and antisocial behavior through their lyrics, lifestyles, and antics on stage. But the influence of these performers was limited to their recordings and occasional appearances on television or in a live concert. Today, however, through MTV, VH-1, and videos, such groups can have an almost instant influence as kids see and hear them over and over. I have seen the effects of this phenomenon first in fashion, as kids emulated their favorite entertainers' clothing and hairstyles, and then in language and lifestyle.

Videos also reinforce and magnify obscene and violent lyrics through the visual images portrayed. In the past, a complaint about rock music was that the words were unintelligible—today we can *see* what the words mean, and very little is left to the imagination. In addition to sexually explicit lyrics, some rap musicians and other performers promote rape, suicide, and murder through their songs.

Other negative societal influences include newspapers, magazines, and books. Sports magazines have their annual swimsuit editions, featuring photographs that would have been considered soft porn a generation ago. Even before children can read, they can be infected by what they hear and see.

In the face of such a host of negative, destructive, anti-Christian influences, parents feel compelled to shield and protect their precious children. This is especially true when our children are toddlers because they haven't yet come face-to-face with the world. They're unspoiled. When a bad scene comes on television, we want to turn off the set . . . forever. And we dread the day that our children will lose their innocence.

We know they will eventually, but usually that fateful event comes sooner than we expect—as soon as they begin to play with other kids. And this is the third passage of parenting—introducing our children to the world.

Even if we were able to shut our families away from the bad videos, movies, music, and news, we wouldn't be able to do the same for other families. My mother-in-law remarked that her children were wonderful and sweet until they went into the neighborhood. She could always tell when Gail had been to a certain neighbor's home by the way she acted when she came home. Until your child plays with other children, all the child knows is your home—that's their whole world. But children from other families introduce your child to different values, behaviors, attitudes, and entertainment. That's what makes this passage so frustrating.

One summer Saturday, Kara came home after playing with a neighborhood friend. I was relaxing in the family room as she passed by me on her way to the bathroom, singing, "Let's get physical. Let me hear your body talk, body talk." I almost fell off the couch. At that moment I realized with sorrow that it would be impossible to shield

Kara from all negative influences. We lived in a nice neighborhood, at the end of a dead-end street in Mandeville, Louisiana. We didn't play that kind of music at home or in the car. And Kara hadn't been to school yet. Kara was about as sheltered from the world as a child can get, but still she was being affected.

Comedian Emo Phillips tells this story: "I remember one day I'll never forget. I was about six and I was playing, and I saw the cellar door open, just a crack. Now, ever since I could remember, my parents had always told me, 'Emo, whatever you do, don't go near the cellar door.' But I had to see what was on the other side if it killed me. And I went to the cellar door, and I pushed it and walked through, and I saw strange, wonderful things, things I had never seen before—like trees, grass, flowers, the sun. . . ."

When our son, Paul, casually used God's name in vain, my wife's and my initial feeling was that the world had corrupted our precious child, and that if the world was going to be that way about it, then we'll just take our boy and go home. We wanted to embrace him and apologize to him and assure him that it wouldn't happen again because he wouldn't set foot outside the house until his wedding day, and even then we'll drive him to the church in an armored personnel carrier to meet his bride for the first time, whom his mother and I will have selected for him.

But of course, it doesn't work that way. The idea is not to insulate children but to equip them—not with our fragile cocoon but with the whole armor of God. Granted, it involves risk and hurt and prayer without ceasing, but isn't that preferable to the cellar scenario?

John Pickerl

⁓⁓⁓⁓⁓⁓⁓⁓⁓⁓⁓⁓⁓⁓⁓⁓⁓⁓

A few years later, I had a similar experience with Dana, although she was a bit older and in school at the time. During our dinner discussion, Kara mentioned how silly a boy had acted at school that day. Dana jokingly remarked, "He must be on drugs." Gail and I were shocked. I hardly knew that drugs existed when I was in *high school,* and then they were always used by some stranger in a faraway city. But there was my young daughter, aware of and discussing such things. David Elkind was right when he wrote that, in this information age, kids can't be kids anymore—they're bombarded by news of the problems in the world and forced to grow up too soon (*All Grown Up & No Place to Go.* Reading, Mass.: Addison-Wesley, 1984).

OTHER VALUES

Let's face it, our children are going to learn about the world's value system—we cannot shelter or shield them forever, nor should we. When a child plays at a friend's house, he will be exposed to that family's values. He will see how the family members relate to each other, he will hear them comment on events in the world, he will observe the interaction between husband and wife and parents and children, he will notice how those parents discipline. Art Wittmann remembers that all of his daughter's friends seemed to come from broken homes. And he was shocked at what some of those parents allowed their children to do. Unfortunately, that will become more and more prevalent as our society devalues marriage.

The child will also be exposed to the other family's values by how his friend plays and behaves. And he will hear and see the background music and TV shows. So don't be shocked when your child begins to imitate her friends and their families.

John and Cindy Pickerl have twin boys. John explains: *One evening after supper, the boys sat at the kitchen table playing with Gak, the modern equivalent of Silly Putty but with greater adhesion to men's dress slacks. Michael completed something and said, "Look what I made," at which Paul expressed his marvel with the phrase, "Oh my God!"*

Cindy and I blinked and gasped and sputtered and said, "Uh, Paul, honey, what did you say?"

"I said, 'Oh my G—'"

"Never mind, Son! Forget we asked! Paul, do you remember when we learned the Ten Commandments?"

"Uh-huh."

"And remember the one with the real funky rhythm?"

"Yeah, that's a cool one!" he responded, and started dancing

*around the kitchen. "'Thou shalt **not** / Take the **name** / **of** the Lord thy **God** in **vain!**' That's my favorite."*

"It's one of mine too," my wife said.

"Definitely within the top three," I noted.

"What does it mean?" Paul asked, in one of those rare moments when the door of rote memory opens to understanding.

"It means saying 'God' when you don't really mean it," I explained. "Like when you're not talking to God or about God."

Paul thought for a minute and said, "So when I pray . . ."

"The Lord loves it," I said.

"And if I say, 'God made the stars . . .'"

"That's good too," his mother replied.

"But if I say, 'Look what Michael made! Oh my God! . . .'"

"That's taking his name 'in vain.'"

John and Cindy were able to teach their sons an important lesson, but in the process they learned one as well: Kids pick up stuff from their friends.

So if we can't totally protect our kids from the world, what can we do?

HOW TO RESPOND

1. Use Common Sense

Acknowledging that we can't totally eliminate outside influences doesn't mean that we surrender and give up our children. Being responsible parents means controlling the television, radio, and other technological intrusions. There's no better time to begin monitoring and limiting television use than when children are young. You'll have a fight on your hands if you try to start when they're in junior high. So I suggest limiting TV viewing, even at this early age.

This includes not using the TV as a baby-sitter. Unfortunately, that's what many parents do because it's easy and convenient. They plop the kids in front of the tube and let them watch the cartoons, *Sesame Street*, or whatever, assuming that the programming is good as long as the kids are quiet. I recently saw a woman on a news report discussing why her two and a half year old started a fire in the house. The woman explained that the child was very impressionable and would copy just about anything he saw on TV. Then she named several shows, including *Beavis and Butt-head, MacGyver,* and others. I wanted to yell at the set, "Why do you let him see those shows? Turn off the set!"

Instead of being used (or abused) by Hollywood through technology, you can use it to help build your family. Many outstanding Christian videos for children are available, as well as tapes and compact discs. And instead of watching television, you can turn off your set and read books to your children. Bookstore shelves overflow with new publications each year that focus kids' attention on Christ and reinforce Christian values.

You can also open your home to your child's friends, thus exposing them to *your* values. Make up an excuse to throw a party; show Christian videos; organize a neighborhood mothers co-op. In other words, find creative ways to be involved with your child and their friends. Darian Veerman says, "As I look back on when the twins were young, I regret not going out and just having fun together."

Myrllis Aycock explains: *We lived in a neighborhood with lots of kids. There weren't moms' groups then. Generally, though, kids came to our house. We had lots of stuff around and invited them over. Even in those days, I was aware of bad things going on with certain children, so they came to our house and played on their Big Wheels. This continued through adolescence. Our house was always a haven. We'd come home from church or wherever, and kids would be in our front yard waiting for us. Every fall, I would have to reseed the backyard because the kids played football in our yard.*

Dear Kelson,

Sometimes I think fathering is a roller-coaster ride. One day you love me; the next day you don't. One day you come when I call you; the next day you ignore my every word. One day you're an angel; the next day you pour half a gallon of water on the bedroom carpet.

Tonight, when you dumped water on the carpet, I wanted to spank and scold you. I figured that if I didn't, you would not know what a bad thing you had done. But you just sat there at the fringe of the puddle, fascinated with it. To you there was no evil in the puddle, just a new experience.

I think my reaction confused you. You could tell I was upset, but you didn't know why. When I yelled and frantically grabbed five towels and soaked up what I could, you saw my frustration and anger.

On days like that, I feel a gnawing uneasiness in

my stomach. I walk around in a daze, asking, "What am I doing wrong?" Those are the times I pray harder than usual.

Then I remember: My job is to train you. "Train a child in the way he should go," says Proverbs 22:6. *That's* what I'm here for—not to make you bullet-proof . . . or perfect.

I would be a better daddy if I remembered that more often. Thank you for forgiving me so easily.

Love, Dad

Daryl Lucas

You can avoid the negative influence of the world by using your creativity and common sense.

2. Teach Truths

Children's experiences with their friends provide great opportunities to teach important truths. For example, suppose Mom prohibits Johnny from doing something, and Johnny protests and says, "But Billy's mom lets him!" Johnny's mother could say, "You're not Billy" and explain that God has given her and Johnny's father the responsibility of raising him, and they have to do what they believe is best. When children come home after playing with friends, take time to talk with them about the experience. If they exhibit attitudes, actions, or language that you don't approve of, let them know how you feel, seriously and firmly.

Your children should know that you take parenting seriously. "We're not perfect—we'll make mistakes. But we love you and thank God every day for you, and we're trying to do our best to raise you the way God wants us to."

Early in the parenting experience it's important to let children know that TV, movies, radio, and so forth are not the final authority. Just because a celebrity says something doesn't mean it's right. The most ridiculous example of the implied authority of the television or movie screen is the advertisement in which a man in a white coat says, "I'm not a doctor, but I play one on TV" and then proceeds to try to sell us over-the-counter medicine.

I've always been fascinated by how people accept whatever is presented on the screen or tube as gospel truth. When a Bible story is dramatized in a movie, people will say, "I didn't know that's the way it was." Instead, they should say, "I wonder if that's accurate. I'll check the Bible and see."

The Bible is the authority, not Hollywood writers, producers, and directors. Don't be afraid to talk back to the TV set, refuting the lies and setting the record straight.

Another teachable moment occurs when children repeat words or phrases that they have heard others say. Similar to what the Pickerls did, you can say that you don't use words like that and explain why. The first time a child utters a forbidden exclamation or epithet, they probably are innocently parroting what a friend said. So don't throw a hissy fit and punish the child. On the other hand, repeat performances should be handled differently.

You also should warn children about what they are likely to encounter in the world. You don't want them to become paranoid or to get a martyr complex, but they should know that there are differences among families—not everyone thinks or lives the way your family does.

Barb Miller feels strongly about this. She says: *If you are a Christian, there will be a pronounced difference between your family and other families. I believe you should be very open with your child about other people's values without prejudicing them against the world. I want my children to know what is right and to act accordingly. This is difficult in the younger years when they want to have friends and are easily influenced. Courtney and I had many discussions with Justin about following what he knew was right, and we punished him when he disobeyed. Now we are going through the same thing with our daughter.*

3. Model Values

Children pick up the values that they see modeled in their world. And these first few years of life are critical for values formation. Therefore, it's important to model the kinds of values you want your children to have. In other words, you should be the kind of person you want your child to be.

I was sitting in my easy chair, holding Dana and playing with her when the phone rang. I quickly put her down and got up to answer the phone. Afterward, I thought about what I had done, what I had communicated to Dana through my actions. If I left her every time the phone rang, I would be telling Dana that a plastic, ringing machine on the wall was more important than she was. That led me to analyze what my other actions might be teaching my little girl. Dana was just a small child, but she could learn from what I did, where I turned my attention, and how I used my time.

I believe that if it is desirable for children to be kind, appreciative, and pleasant, those qualities should be taught—not hoped for. If we want to see honesty, truthfulness, and unselfishness in our offspring, then these characteristics should be the conscious objectives of our early instructional process. If it is important to produce respectful, responsible young citizens, then we should set out to mold them accordingly. The point is obvious: *heredity does not equip a child with proper attitudes; children learn what they are taught.* We cannot expect the coveted behavior to appear magically if we have not done our early homework.

Dr. James Dobson, The New Dare to Discipline (Wheaton, Ill.: Tyndale House, 1992), pp. 14–15.

Think about the values you model at home. What do your children think is important to you? Are *they* on your list? And what about your spouse and the family as a whole? By their interest and investment of time, many parents demonstrate that their job or career ranks far ahead of marriage, family, and children. You model that your kids are important to you by spending time with them—having fun together, playing, talking, and listening. You show that you value marriage and love your spouse by displaying affection for your partner in front of the kids. You can model the value of family by establishing family traditions and holding regular celebrations. You can demonstrate the importance of the individual child by doing something special and fun with just that child. Your children hold a very high place in your heart—show it.

You also should model the importance of God, church, and the Bible. From their earliest years, your children should realize that your relationship with God is a vital part of your lives. Many times my parents would try to have regular family devotions. With five kids ranging in age from three to sixteen and several complicated schedules to coordinate, Mom and Dad's attempts were usually short-lived. So I don't remember much of what we covered—but I do remember that they tried. Also, we had a map on the kitchen wall, right next to the table where we ate all our meals. My folks had placed pictures of several missionaries on this map in the countries where they served. From time to time we would pray for specific missionaries and their needs. At every meal I was reminded of these men and women who were serving God around the world. Even if we didn't take time to pray, I would see the map.

Myrllis Aycock says: *We made an issue of prayer and God's answers. The boys learned incredible things from seeing God meet our needs. In Youth for Christ, we didn't always have a steady paycheck. But time after time, God met the need we had for groceries and other essentials. Often we would return from church on Sunday night, and sitting in front of the door would be a bag of food. We came home one night, and the lights were all on in the house. The side door and the back door were both open. We went in cautiously, and someone was putting food in the refrigerator for us. Those situations made indelible impressions on our children.*

You can model the value of prayer by praying often (alone and with the family) and by praying individually with each child. You can show that the Bible is important to you by having a personal, daily quiet time, by memorizing Bible verses together as a family, and by hosting home Bible studies. You can demonstrate the importance of the church through regular attendance at worship services and by your involvement in other church activities and responsibilities.

Include your children with you in church activities whenever possible. Jim and Kathe Galvin explain: *An important part of exposing kids to the outside world is to give them meaningful experiences in church. We signed our children up for children's choir, Sunday school, and child care during Women's Bible Study, and we brought them with us to church potluck dinners.* Children learn how to love God by watching their parents.

We have three children, ages four, five, and six. (Fertility is not a problem for us, and family planning is not our strong suit!) I am a speech/language pathologist who specializes in the special needs of pediatric patients. I see many kids and work with lots of parents. I know tons about child development and behavior modification, and find myself giving advice

all the time on child rearing and dealing with problems. Therefore, I thought I would make a great parent. What has really thrown me is how quickly all
my education and knowledge went out the window.
When it comes to my own kids, my parenting re-
verts back to the style my mother used. What is
even more shocking is that I do the very things I absolutely hated that she did. It is not that the techniques I suggest to other parents don't work—they
do. It is me. I'm not a bad parent, but the creative,
intellectual parent that I thought I would be is so
easily replaced by the emotional, knee-jerk, reaction-
ary parent.

Patty Atkins

Another way to teach positive values is to take quick
action against negative ones. Let's say that there's an incident
in the neighborhood, at church, or in a friend's family that
is clearly wrong (for example, one child beats up another, a
husband deserts his family, or a driver curses you out).
Without condemning specific individuals, you should speak
the truth to your children and then explain your reasoning.
And when you do or say something wrong, you should be
quick to admit your mistake and, if necessary, ask for for-
giveness. Children learn right and wrong from listening to
you and from watching you live.

The initial surprise at this parenting passage is that the
child is being affected by the world, by people whose life-

styles and values differ greatly from yours. Initially, and quite naturally, you may react by trying to shield the child, protecting them from all outsiders and their evil influences completely. But that's impossible. Instead, by *using common sense, teaching truths,* and *modeling values,* you help the child understand the world and how to live in it.

LET'S THINK ABOUT IT

Warnings

- *Don't overreact* by trashing the TV, punishing a child for repeating a bad word, banning a neighborhood child from your house, etc.
- *Don't try to shelter your child from all outside influences.* It's impossible, impractical, and inappropriate.
- *Don't condemn your child's friends and their families.* Instead, model and teach the characteristics of a good family.

Opportunities

- *Teach truths about God and his Word.* Let your child know, for example, that God wants them to be involved *in* the world, not separate from it (see John 17:15).
- *Encourage communication with your child.* Let them know that they can tell you anything and that you will listen without interrupting, overreacting, or judging before having all the facts.
- *Watch for teachable moments.* Use your child's experiences with other children and their families to help you

teach them valuable lessons about life, God, family, and being a Christian in the real world.

- *Pray for God's protection over your child,* every day.
- *Invite your child's friends to play at your house.* Be creative in planning parties and other activities.
- *Model godly values in your home.* Show your child what real Christians are like.

Lessons

- *Parents cannot totally shield and protect their children from negative influences in the world.* We should teach our children to deal with the world as it is and not retreat from it.
- *Parents should be responsible and do their best, but still they must trust God.* God is in control.
- *Many of a child's basic values are learned and shaped during these early years of life.* We should spend time with our children, loving them, teaching them, and pointing them to Christ.

Resources

- Chuck Aycock and Dave Veerman, *From Dad with Love* (Wheaton, Ill.: Tyndale House, 1994). Through their experience as fathers and with the help of the National Center for Fathering, the authors tell how dads can give gifts to their children: protection, confidence, and identity—gifts that money can't buy.
- Kimberley Converse and Richard G. Hagstrom, *The Myth of the Perfect Mother* (Eugene, Oreg.: Harvest

House, 1993). This very practical book tells how to be a great mom without being perfect and shows mothers how to adjust their parenting styles to fit kids' individual personalities.

◆ Dr. James Dobson, *The New Dare to Discipline* (Wheaton, Ill.: Tyndale House, 1992). This classic book (originally published in 1970) gives a wealth of advice on why and how to discipline children in order to help them grow into responsible adults.

◆ *The Eager Reader Bible* (Wheaton, Ill.: Tyndale House, 1994). This book offers a fully illustrated journey through the Bible with the main stories retold in language that children can easily understand. Parents can give this to their eager readers or read from it to even younger children.

◆ *Focus on the Family* is a Christian organization devoted to preserving and strengthening families. Their monthly magazine contains several helpful articles, and their daily radio broadcasts offer invaluable insight and counsel on a variety of issues that touch the family. They also produce and distribute a number of outstanding books, videotapes, and other resources. For more information, write to P.O. Box 35500, Colorado Springs, CO 80935-3550, or call 719-531-3400.

◆ *McCullough Family Media, Inc.* The purpose of this company is to provide a variety of value-oriented films from a Christian perspective that entertain all ages. They produce their own movies, distribute others, and publish a monthly newsletter/order form. For more information, write to 2924 Knight St., Shreveport, LA 71105, or call 800-259-2226.

♦ Michael J. McManus, *50 Practical Ways to Take Our Kids Back from the World* (Wheaton, Ill.: Tyndale House, 1993). As the title indicates, this book is filled with practical advice for parents to help them teach their children to live with Christian values in the world.

♦ *Mothers of Preschoolers International (MOPS)* is an organization that works through local churches to provide support to mothers of young children. Each bimonthly meeting features a coffee time, a speaker, and then discussion and crafts. Baby-sitting is available. MOPS has also been very successful at reaching out to women in the community. A leader of the group in one church reports that 75 percent of the mothers who come do not attend that church. For more information, write to 1311 S. Clarkson St., Denver, CO 80210, or call 303-733-5353.

♦ Kenneth N. Taylor, *Family-Time Bible in Pictures* (Wheaton, Ill.: Tyndale House, 1992). This book contains 128 Bible stories, retold by Dr. Taylor and illustrated with dramatic and realistic artwork. Ideal for family devotions.

Sending Your Child to School

~

4

The wheels on the bus go round and round
round and round
round and round.
The wheels on the bus go round and round
all through the town.

The driver on the bus says, "Move on back"
"Move on back"

"Move on back."
The driver on the bus says, "Move on back"
all through the town.

My daughters and I sang that little song dozens of times, each time adding new verses about the windshield wipers on the bus, the kids on the bus, the lights on the bus, and so forth. We laughed and sang and generally had a great time . . . until they actually had to get on one of those big yellow buses and be driven to school. Suddenly I wasn't very confident about the ability of the driver of the bus and the safety of the bus—wheels, windshield wipers, lights, and everything else! That bus was taking my darling daughters away from me.

Many parents agree that one of the most traumatic of the parenting passages is this fourth one—sending the child off to school for the first time.

In his wonderful book *Six Hours One Friday,* Max Lucado describes his and his wife's experience as they anticipated their daughter Jenna's first day of school:

> *For four lightning-fast years she'd been ours, and ours alone. And now that was all going to change.*
>
> *We'd put her to bed last night as "our girl"—exclusive property of Mommy and Daddy. Mommy and Daddy read to her, taught her, listened to her. But beginning today, someone else would, too.*
>
> *Until today, it was Mommy and Daddy who wiped*

away the tears and put on the Band-Aids. But beginning today, someone else would, too.

I didn't want to wake her.

Until today, her life was essentially us—Mom, Dad, and baby sister Andrea. Today that life would grow—new friends, a teacher. Her world was this house—her room, her toys, her swing set. Today her world would expand. She would enter the winding halls of education—painting, reading, calculating . . . becoming.

I didn't want to wake her. Not because of the school. It's a fine one. Not because I don't want her to learn. Heaven knows I want her to grow, to read, to mature. Not because she doesn't want to go. School has been all she could talk about for the last week!

No, I didn't want to wake her up because I didn't want to give her up. (Portland, Oreg.: Multnomah, 1989, pp. 47–48)

Lucado describes what most parents feel as they send their children off to school: insecurity, fear, and sadness. And parents are surprised by those feelings as what was supposed to be an exciting day begins to fill them with anxiety and dread.

I see it every year at the end of August because I live next to an elementary school. On the first day of school, parents parade past my home with their little ones in tow. Dressed up for the important first day, most of the children seem excited about the prospect. A few, however, cry and don't want to leave Mommy or Daddy. Many of the parents wield video cameras, and all of them seem a little saddened as they say good-bye to their children and then turn and walk away. It's often tougher for parents than for their children.

Myrllis Aycock reports: *I remember the day we sent Craig off to kindergarten. He needed to walk across a busy street, down the block, and across another busy street. There were crossing guards at each street. When we got outside, meeting all the moms and dads, Craig looked at me and said, "Mom, I'm fine. You don't need to go with me." I felt a stab in my heart. Then I said, "Well, I'll just walk behind. This is the first day, so I'll just walk behind—I'd like to do that." After that, he walked with the other kids.*

Babs Swanson also expresses her difficulties in this passage: *I felt I was no longer able to **carefully** choose Brooke's environment. I felt as if Dave and I were **thrusting her out** into the cold, cruel world.*

I wanted to send her off each day "right." I remember one winter day when I knelt down in front of her and told her that I loved her, that Jesus loved her and was with her, how precious she was . . . and she interrupted me and said, "Mom, your teeth are yellow—could be plaque." So much for that special moment!

IT'S TIME TO GO TO SCHOOL

As we prepare our kids for their first encounter with school, our first surprise is realizing how quickly time is passing. We will become even more painfully aware of this as our children progress through the school years.

The toddler and elementary school years should be seen as fleeting opportunities. Yet this priceless period of influence often occurs at a time when fathers are the least accessible to their kids.

Dr. James Dobson, Straight Talk to Men and Their Wives (Dallas: Word, 1980, 1984), p. 34.

Someone has said that from birth to about third grade seems to take thirty years, and from third grade to college graduation seems to take three minutes. This is because the first few years of life are filled with intensive involvement in the child's life—changing diapers, feeding, burping, cleaning up, dressing, carrying, playing with, giving a bath, putting to bed, giving medicine, comforting, teaching to walk, helping to talk, protecting, and on and on. When babies and toddlers are awake, we're afraid to let them out of our sight for fear of what they might get into. Little children exhaust our supplies of time and energy.

During the elementary school years, however, things change. Children become more independent: walking to a neighbor's house to play, going to the park, riding a bike, making a snowman in the backyard *on their own.* And they become increasingly involved outside the home, taking lessons and participating in choirs, athletic teams, and any number of activities offered by the community and private groups. Because of all the families and activities in my city,

owning a minivan and a video camera seem like require-
ments for citizenship. On a typical fall or spring Saturday,
every park is jammed with kids' soccer teams and their
proud parents who record every move on tape.

During these years, Mom and Dad become chauffeurs,
shuttling kids between home and practices, lessons, games,
and performances. Even during adolescence, after the kids
get their driver's licenses and can drive themselves to practices and games, there's no letup in the family's frantic pace
because the number of activities increases. Multiply busy
schedules by the number of kids in the family, and you can
see why the days fly by. Parents begin to feel the increasing
pace—beginning with kindergarten.

Children Are Changing

Parents are also surprised by how quickly time passes because they can see the dramatic changes in their children. As
we send them off to kindergarten, we dress them up as boys
and girls—and we realize that they're not babies anymore.
Then we get out their baby books and reminisce about their
first few weeks and months of life. We know that we've
prepared them for this moment, but it seems like just
yesterday we were bringing them home from the hospital.

Our twins were five years old and in different kindergarten classes. One day at dinner, Brandon prayed,
"Dear God, bless our food. Bless our family. Bless the
poor people and help them have enough to eat and a

place to sleep. And Lord, bless our shelter. Now God, Crystal probably doesn't know what shelter means. It's a house, God; it's a home; it's where we live." As Brandon continued his prayer, making sure that God realized that he was just a bit smarter than his twin sister, Crystal interrupted, "Tell him, God, that I know what a shelter is 'cause I'm in kindergarten, too!"

Bill Sanders

At five and six years old, our children are talking fluently and may even be reading. If they have older brothers and sisters, they have copied their behavior as they have tried to look and act older.

As I mentioned in the last chapter, in this age of information, children are painfully aware of what is going on in the world. Even positive children's shows feature public-service announcements about drug and alcohol abuse and avoiding strangers. Don't misunderstand me—those announcements need to be made. Unfortunately, the condition of our world necessitates that we communicate such information to young children. But that's just the point: Children can't be children any more. They look at a milk carton, see the face of a kidnapped child, and realize that the world contains many evil, dangerous people. As we send them off to school, we remind them not to talk to strangers and to come straight home afterwards.

So it seems as though they are growing up before our eyes.

Life Is Short

Another reason that we're surprised by our feelings during this passage is that it may be our first realization of the brevity of life. Job 14:5 states, "You have set mankind so brief a span of life—months is all you give him! Not one bit longer may he live" (TLB).

A youthful misconception is that time is a constant and that life is long. When we were very young, for example, we couldn't even think of waiting a year for anything—Christmas seemed so far away. That's because a year was a relatively large percentage of our lifetimes. I remember an eighth grade history teacher commenting that an event happened *only ten years ago.* And I thought, *Only ten years ago! That's a long time!* And it was to me because ten years represented more than two-thirds of my life to that point. As we age, however, a year is a smaller and smaller portion of our lives; thus the years seem to fly by. Now it's easy for me to say or think, *Only ten years ago.* In fact, I find myself having to count up how many years I've been married and how old my kids are. And each year as I put up my Christmas decorations, I feel as though I just took them down from the previous Christmas.

Most of the parents of kindergartners (especially the eldest child) are young—in their twenties or early thirties. So they haven't yet experienced much of life. Seeing the child go to school awakens them to the reality of the brevity of life. Where has the time gone?

Years ago, my friend Jim Green told me that he and his wife, Judy, had just figured out that they would have their daughter at home for only about half the time that she was up and about. She had just turned nine. That realization came as a shock to them. Jim's comment made me reflect on my time with my children: "They grow up so fast. How can I be a better parent? What should I do to invest my life in them? How can I make the most of the time we will have together?" The time passes much too quickly.

Having twins, Darian and I were ready for them to go to school. We saw school as a help. But during those years, I had to travel a lot on business and was out of town during the week, so I wasn't able to be there when they came home. When I returned from a trip, it would take a day for Erik and Crista to adjust to their dad.

Paul Veerman

IT'S TIME *TO GO* TO SCHOOL

The second surprise in sending our children to their first day of school is the sadness at letting them go. Of course we haven't released them completely (that will come much later), but this is the first step in that process. We know it and we feel it.

Up to this point, our children have been all ours, and they've been totally dependent on us. Everything has centered around our homes and families. We have fed them nearly every meal, read them nearly every story, transported them every place, and taught them nearly every lesson. We've been their best friends and confidants. For almost every second of their lives, we have known what they were doing, where, and with whom. But starting now, their world will expand, as will their vision and dreams. When they come home, they will talk about classes and school activities and friends and what happened on the playground. In a couple of years they will want to go on field trips and slumber parties. They will want to teach us. And they will begin to think, question, and argue. In essence, our children will begin to become independent persons—individuals. We want that to happen, but it feels funny and makes us nervous.

My wife and I have found that before each major step in our children's lives, we have a number of fears that later prove to be unfounded. We were scared to death about kindergarten, but Sara, and two years later her brother Stephen, had a great experience. Next we heard all of the terrible things to expect when children go to middle school, but so far, she's doing well there, too. Teaching children the value of taking risks while learning at the same time how to take risks together, with them, can be a real challenge.

Doug Knox

Sally Loan reflects: *Before Amanda went to kindergarten, we had shared **all** her experiences and had a common frame of* *reference. I could always connect with her feelings and thoughts. After school began, I became totally unaware of much of her day. I also found that she was forming opinions that came from sources other than those to which we **chose** to expose her. It was an uncomfortable feeling.*

Letting go for the first time also raises concerns for the child's safety. As I mentioned earlier, we were living in Louisiana when Dana was born and when Kara started school. The school was a few miles away, so usually Kara would take the school bus that picked kids up at the end of our street. I remember watching Kara walk down the street toward the bus stop a few blocks away. She seemed so small and vulnerable. Even when Gail or I would drive Kara to the bus stop and see her board the bus, we would have the same anxieties about her safety. But that is also part of letting go—realizing that we can't be with the child constantly, keeping her safe and secure.

I think Brooke was in third grade when I realized that her successes were *her* successes, her failures were *her* failures, but partly my fault. She is her own person, not an extension of me, but with her own gifts, needs, wants, and dreams, and the sooner I encouraged her individuality, the stronger we both would be.

Babs Swanson

Good parents are concerned for the well-being of their child. Patty Atkins, remembering when her oldest child was six years old and starting kindergarten, says: *What a rude awakening for Tim and me. The world is not the same as it was when we grew up. Adam is supposed to walk to our neighborhood school, approximately half a mile away. However, it is doubtful that we will ever let him walk there. Because of the nearby high school traffic and the general state of the world, he will not know the joy of meandering through the neighborhood. At his age, I had total freedom to roam my neighborhood. My siblings and I would be out and about all day. My kids have to have every activity screened. It makes me sad, and it makes me wonder how isolated my grandchildren will be.*

Years ago, when I rocked Kara to sleep, I would sing this simple song to her:

Kara, oh Kara—
Kara, I love you so.
You are my precious girl
I'll never let you go!

That last line about *never letting go* I didn't mean literally, of course—or did I? The process began in kindergarten and continues . . . and it's tough. But eventually it is time *to go* and for me to *let go*. As they have become more independent, my girls still need Gail and me, but not the same way as in those early years. If they did, something would be terribly wrong with them and with our parenting efforts.

With each year comes more and more independence, and it begins in this fourth passage, when we send them to school.

IT'S TIME TO GO *TO SCHOOL*

The third surprise during this passage of parenting is our anxiety about the school. Until now, Mom and Dad have been the dominant sources of information, counsel, and guidance. Suddenly teachers enter the child's life—for most of each day they will influence them. In most elementary schools, children have the same teacher for all of their classes. In kindergarten that's three hours or so; it's six hours for the other grades. So during the school year, the teacher exerts tremendous influence.

According to the "Family in America" survey conducted in February 1992 by the Barna Research Group, Ltd., here's how the 1,009 people interviewed in the study answered the question, Who or which *should* have the most influence on our children?

Parents	97%
Churches	2%
Schools	1%
Friends and peers of the child	*
The media	*
Government policies	0%

(* denotes less than one-half of one percent)

Compare those figures with the way the same people answered the question: Who or which *does* have the most influence?

Parents	30%
Churches	1%
Schools	13%
Friends and peers of the child	33%
The media	21%
Government policies	1%

George Barna, The Future of the American Family (Chicago: Moody Press, 1992), p. 101.

~~~~~~~~~~

Then there is the issue of peers. The concerns that surfaced during the last passage reappear, only worse. We think of peer pressure, cliques, and playground bullies.

Our worries and concerns about school are exacerbated by what we read and hear about schools today. Reported incidents that, in reality, are isolated and scattered tend to become concentrated in our minds, so we imagine our public school filled with gangs, drugs, sex, administrators who hate Christians, and teachers who promote atheism, New Age philosophy, evolution, humanism, the occult, and moral relativism.

Actually, most public school administrators are decent, conscientious, responsible, and moral people. In my work with Youth for Christ/Campus Life, I spent countless hours on many high school and junior high school campuses.

Obviously, no school is perfect, but none of the schools fit the caricature that many parents imagine. Both of my daughters attended public elementary, middle, and high schools in Illinois and Louisiana. Without exception, Gail and I have been pleased with the quality of the people in charge. In addition, despite the current trend to remove religion from public education, the schools enjoyed a positive relationship with area churches and Christian organizations.

Of course, the quality of the education always boils down to the teacher in the classroom. Here Gail and I have experienced some variations in competence and commitment, but still we have been pleased with most of our children's teachers.

There is cause for concern about America's public schools, especially in light of some of the proposed curriculum, celebrated court cases, declining test scores, and the National Education Association agendas. But we shouldn't despair. Instead, we should get involved, especially if we encounter seemingly incompetent, inexperienced, or unfair teachers. Schools need and welcome volunteers, especially parents, who will chaperone, monitor, sponsor, assist teachers, and help in other ways. And we shouldn't be afraid to voice concerns to administrators and teachers. Communication is vital.

Occasions will arise when the child hears (or thinks he hears) something in class that contradicts what he has been taught at home or in church. Each incident provides another opportunity to teach, to work through the issue with the child. Julie Essenburg says that one day her son Ben came home from kindergarten and said, "You know what my teacher told me? That the hair on our heads came from monkeys who we came from! Isn't that silly!" Julie and Ben were able to discuss what the teacher probably meant and what the Bible says about the origin of human beings.

Instead of worrying or panicking, we should get involved in our kids' lives and become partners with teachers in educating them.

Many families choose to educate their children at home, at least for the first few years. That was the choice of Barb and Courtney Miller. Barb explains: *It is not something that we plan on doing until college. We just take each year at a time. We evaluate each child's needs each year and decide how they can best be met. Another influence in this decision was that we had just adopted a baby and didn't want Justin to feel as though we were kicking him out of the house.*

Others send their children to Christian schools or other private educational institutions. You may prefer one of these options instead of the public school. But if you choose a private school, Christian or otherwise, don't assume that you won't have any of the struggles associated with the first day of school or any of the typical school problems—everything I have said about *time* and *letting go* still applies. And you ought to get involved there, too.

Public, private, or home school? At kindergarten, you can't put off the decision any longer. No more riding the fence. We were fortunate to have a no-lose situation, or so we thought. We had a wonderful public school within walking distance, three Christian schools about equal distance away, and the opportunity to home school since Kathe did not work outside the home. Unfortunately, our friends' opinions about how we should handle our children's education were split about equally among all three options. No matter what we decided, we were going to risk the disapproval of about two-thirds of them. By home schooling our son for kindergarten and sending our daughter to kindergarten at the public school two years later, we succeeded in confusing or irritating nearly everybody. But we thought carefully about which environment would be best for each child as an individual, and we didn't worry about what others might think of us as parents. The result was a wonderful kindergarten year for both children.

Jim Galvin

———

Some parents choose a Christian school and then seem to pull back from their children. It's as though they are saying to the administrators and teachers, "Here's my child. He's yours now to teach, correct, and shape. I expect that you will produce a fine Christian young person. I'll see you at the end of the year." These parents are shocked when their child meets less-than-desirable kids at the Christian school, disobeys and resists their authority, or exhibits otherwise normal behavior at every stage of his growth.

When we send our children off to school, starting with

kindergarten, we *do* relinquish some of the teaching responsibilities to others and we *do* begin to let go. It's a difficult passage but a necessary one if our children are to mature. It's all part of growing up!

HOW TO RESPOND

1. Seize the Moment

Because life is short and our time with our children is quickly passing, we should make the most of the time together. In other words, our children must be a priority in our lives. There is no greater responsibility for parents—children should be right at the top of our list of values. Keeping them there becomes increasingly difficult because with each year of their lives, they will be more involved outside of the home and moving away from us.

Also, during these grade school years, most parents are at the age when their careers put them under tremendous stress. The company may require long hours, weekly business trips, or frequent relocations. Families live in my community for an average of two and a half years, and I have found that the most transient families have preschool and elementary school children.

Making children a top priority will take intentional effort and tough decisions. I know parents who turned down nice promotions and moves to other cities because they wouldn't disrupt their families' lives again. I know parents who have changed jobs in order to have more time with their kids. My brother Phil has a job that requires him to travel quite a bit.

So he intentionally carves out time for his three young children. Often he will take the whole family when he travels to a resort setting. He also coaches the soccer teams of the two oldest kids.

Of course, just being home doesn't guarantee that Mom or Dad will concentrate on their children. Hobbies, television, housework, and even the newspaper can compete for attention. Again, focusing on children may necessitate making difficult decisions. My father loved to play golf, but he gave up the game when it became obvious to him that golf was taking him away from home too often. When my youngest brother left home, Dad took up the sport again. He made an important choice based on his family values.

Nelson Bennett says that one of his greatest regrets is that he didn't *waste* enough time with his kids: *I spent time with them, but we were always doing activities, not always relating. When my son got married, I realized that those days were gone—I didn't have a chance to waste time with him any more, at least not in the same way. However, I look forward to doing this with my grandchildren. And with Theo and Lynn, whenever I can, to catch up.*

How important are your children to you? When they begin to go to school, you will begin to see them less and less. Think of what you can do to spend time with them: playing games, going to sporting events and theatrical productions, helping with schoolwork, telling jokes, reading the Bible, coaching, teaching, talking, or just *wasting time.* Time is short—your kids need you.

2. Loosen the Grip

Because going to kindergarten signals the beginning of our children's move toward eventual independence, we need to begin to prepare ourselves and them for that day.

Darian Veerman advises: *You have to know your kids well enough to know when they're ready to spread their wings. But when they're ready, jump on it! I'm thinking specifically of sleepovers, camp, and other activities. Camp was big for our twins. When an opportunity to go to church camp came up, Crista was excited about going, but Erik wasn't interested at all. Crista went and had a great time. A few years later, Erik was ready and he went to Honey Rock Camp, several hundred miles away. He loved it and his faith grew tremendously.*

Loosening the grip involves thinking through what kind of people we want our children to become and then building into family life whatever it will take to get them there. We should consider each area of life.

Physical

The physical area includes health, conditioning, growth, coordination, and general care of the body. To help your child develop physically, think through diet, activity, hygiene, and sports. It's not too early to teach good eating and sleeping habits and basic hygiene. And involvement in sports and other active play will help children stay physically fit and become coordinated.

Mental

This area includes thinking, reasoning, and understanding.

To help your children develop mentally, you can help them read and choose books and computer games that will have a positive impact and will stretch their minds. Encourage your children with schoolwork and help them develop a thirst for learning. Take their questions seriously, listen carefully, and help them find answers.

Social

Essentially, this area involves building relationships and interacting with others. With your child's first school encounter will come a host of relational challenges. Be prepared to teach your child how to find friends, be a good friend, and resolve conflicts. This is also the ideal time to have new friends from school over to your house. Get to know the friends' parents as well. Your goal should be to encourage your child to build positive friendships.

According to the parents and kids we surveyed, these were the top sources of conflict *before the teen years*:

- Wanting to spend time with their friends
- Fighting with siblings
- Not doing what they're told
- Outright disobedience
- Being selfish
- Their will vs. your will
- Trouble at school
- Talking back

- Not listening to directions
- Breaking rules
- Temper tantrums
- Using "that tone of voice"
- Telling lies or half-truths

Greg Johnson and Mike Yorkey, Faithful Parents, Faithful Kids (Wheaton, Ill.: Tyndale House, 1993), p. 22.

This is also the time to teach your child about making moral decisions. Larry Kreider tells about when his daughter Erica was invited to a sleepover. He and Susan had given permission for her to go: *We were eating dinner that Friday evening before Erica went to her girlfriend's home, and we were discussing the party. I asked what would happen at the party. Erica answered, "Well, after everyone gets there, we're going to watch a movie. Then after the movie, we'll have some popcorn, play games, and other stuff." So I asked, "What movie?" She told me the title, but I didn't recognize it. But Brett, my son who is four years older, did. The movie was R-rated.*

Now I had a dilemma. Erica started to get teary eyed, thinking that we wouldn't allow her to go to her friend's house. So I gave her this option. "You can take games with you, and when they are ready to show the movie, you can play the games by yourself or with any of your friends who want to. But you are not going to see that movie."

At first she thought I was terrible, but then she agreed to take the games with her. I explained that I was trusting her not to watch the movie and I would ask her in the morning. She said she understood.

The next morning I went to pick Erica up, and I asked her what happened. She answered, "Well, I told Mrs. Johnson that I wasn't going to watch the movie, that I was going to play some games instead. And the mother said, 'You know, it probably isn't real good if we show this anyway. Why don't we all play games?' And they never showed the movie."

Larry was able to teach Erica a valuable lesson about right and wrong and about sticking to her convictions with her friends.

Spiritual

Church, Bible reading, prayer, and devotions are all part of spiritual development. As a Christian parent, you should always be focusing on this area in your home, but it becomes even more important as your child grows in their ability to read and think. How much does your child understand of the gospel? What are they learning in Sunday school and in other church activities?

This is the ideal time to begin having family devotions. Gail and I found that Kara and Dana loved teaching *us* their Sunday school lessons, and we had fun memorizing Scripture together as a family.

One of the greatest thrills parents can have is leading a child to Christ. Gail and I both had that wonderful opportunity with our girls. I remember being very sensitive to this issue with Dana. I knew I could scare or pressure her into going through some spiritual motions, reciting a prayer to "accept Jesus into her heart," but I didn't want to do that. I wanted Dana to make her own decision based on her knowledge and understanding of Christ. So every night as we prayed together at bedtime, I would include bits of the gospel story in my prayer. My hope was that Dana would pick up on the clues and ask questions. I remember praying, "And I thank you most of all for Jesus, who died on the cross for our sins so that we might have eternal life." One night, when Gail followed me into Dana's room to pray with her, Dana asked, "What's going to happen to the turtle?" When Gail asked what she meant, Dana responded, "Well, Daddy prayed about the 'turtle's life,' so I just wondered." When I heard Dana's comment, I realized that she wasn't yet ready to make her personal commitment to Christ. But eventually that day arrived, and I had the great thrill of leading her to the Savior.

Consider how you are helping your child mature and grow in all of these areas. Think about where you want your child to be physically, mentally, socially, and spiritually. Then work with your spouse to move your child in that direction.

3. Support the School

Because this is your child's first experience with school, you should help them enjoy the experience. Although you may have fears and concerns about school, don't voice them and thus frighten your child. You want them to look forward to class and to develop a thirst for learning. So emphasize the positive aspects of the educational experience. If you have questions and concerns, take them to the teacher or principal.

As I mentioned earlier, you should also look for ways to get involved in the school. Gail volunteered every year as a teacher's aide at our elementary school. I couldn't spend those hours there, but I was in charge of the school's Fun Fair for three years. Both of us were very careful to attend every open house and school program. Over the years we enjoyed very good communication with our daughters' teachers and the schools' administrations.

Myrllis Aycock says: *I didn't really trust people, especially people that didn't know the Lord. So entrusting my son to a teacher was a big thing for me. I became involved, got to know the teacher, became a room mom, went on field trips, and so forth. The more I did, the more I relaxed about those kinds of issues.*

Think of what you can do to become involved in your child's school. In addition to enhancing communication, your presence will affirm the importance of school to your child.

Sending your child off to school for the first time can be much more scary for you than for your child. You know that it is a significant milestone in the child's life and a signal that they are growing up. But during this passage you can spend time with your child, helping them develop *physically, mentally, socially,* and *spiritually.* And you can become involved in the educational process, communicating with teachers and volunteering your time, energy, and expertise to the school.

LET'S THINK ABOUT IT

Warnings

- *Don't panic about how fast your child is growing up.* Let this realization spur you to get more involved with the child.
- *Don't create an emotional scene as you send your child to school.* You will only make it more difficult for them. It's time to begin letting your child go.
- *Don't believe all the horror stories you hear about public schools.* Most schools are not nearly as bad as you hear.
- *Don't scare your child by warning them excessively about the dangers in school.* You want your child to enjoy school and to learn.

Opportunities

- *Take advantage of the time you have with your children—* you need *quantity* as well as *quality* time. Change your schedule and rearrange your activities to make your children a top priority.
- *Help build your child's excitement about school and learning* by reading books together, talking over what they learned in school, and prominently displaying their schoolwork.
- *Use discussion about incidents at school as teachable moments.* Notes from a teacher, grades, conflicts on the playground, awards, and punishments—all can be used as discussion starters.
- *Work in partnership with the school in teaching your child.*

Volunteer at the school, become involved in the parent-teacher association, and get to know your child's teachers.

Lessons

- *Time passes quickly and our children grow up fast* (see James 4:14). We shouldn't continually put off the special activities that we want to do as a family and with each child.

- *It's tough to begin letting go of our children, but we must*—that's a part of growing up (see 1 Corinthians 13:11). But we can help our children grow in the right direction (see Proverbs 22:6).

- *Just as he is with us, God is with our children, even at school* (see Romans 8:38-39 and Hebrews 13:5).

Resources

- Jay Kesler, Ron Beers, and LaVonne Neff, eds., *Parents and Children* (Wheaton, Ill.: Victor, 1986). This seven-hundred-page volume is a virtual encyclopedia of information covering just about every child-rearing topic. Hundreds of articles by scores of writers provide a wealth of practical, Christ-centered advice.

- *Kids Application Bible* (Wheaton, Ill.: Tyndale House, 1994). This is a special edition of the best-selling and award-winning *Life Application Bible.* Designed for elementary-age children, it is packed with features that will help them dig into God's Word and apply it to their lives.

◆ Dave Veerman, *The One Year Bible Memory Book for Families* (Wheaton, Ill.: Tyndale House, 1993). This book will help families memorize Scripture together and is ideal for family devotions. A different verse is presented each week, printed in three popular Bible translations (the King James Version, *The Living Bible,* and the New International Version), and each day an application note is given, drawn from the featured verse for that week.

◆ David R. Veerman, James C. Galvin, James C. Wilhoit, Daryl J. Lucas, and Richard Osborne, *101 Questions Children Ask about God* (Wheaton, Ill.: Tyndale House, 1992) and *102 Questions Children Ask about the Bible* (Wheaton, Ill.: Tyndale House, 1994). Featuring honest questions asked by real children (for example: "If God made spiders, why do people squish them?" and "Does God sleep or does he just rest?"), these books contain thoughtful answers, key verses from *The Simplified Living Bible,* notes to parents, and related questions.

Hitting
Adolescence

5

Clickity-click, *clickity-click* . . . the car moves quickly forward. *Clickity-click, clickity-click* . . . continuing along, then slower as the grade steepens. *Clickity-click, clickity-click* . . . steel on steel, higher and higher, until riders see only blue sky and clouds. Then over the crest and suddenly downward, the car hurtles toward the earth, pushing belted passengers hard into the seat backs with breath caught in their throats. Joyful screams and rushing wind muffle all other sounds. Quickly to the right, then up . . . and down, sharply left, up again . . . then down and around, upside down and up . . . to the right and a corkscrew, then down . . . and coasting to the station . . . *clickity-click, clickity-click.*

Roller coasters pack sixty seconds of thrills into every minute. And despite the stomach-churning, breathtaking experience, excited amusement-park patrons pay and patiently wait for their opportunity to ride. It's great once . . . or twice . . . or even three times. But what if you were subjected to days and weeks of almost continuous ups, downs, and stomach flip-flops? Most people would quickly tire of the experience and beg to be released.

Yet that's what many parents feel every day.

Trish slinks down the stairs, five minutes after having been called to dinner. Sullen and downcast, she sneers at Dad when he questions her tardiness. A minute or so later, she giggles and laughs almost uncontrollably as she relates a recent conversation between Marci and Herschel. Suddenly she announces her hatred for *stupid* school, especially Mrs. Grant, her English teacher. And that's just the beginning. During the rest of the meal, Trish exhibits sadness about a relationship, excitement about a boy, happiness about her plans for the weekend, anger at her brother's comment, and laughter at a silly joke. A roller coaster ride of emotions. The ride is not solo—the whole family is with her, and they don't like it. In fact, they are exhausted and sick of the whole thing.

Is Trish psychotic? On drugs? Suffering from lack of sleep?

No, Trish is simply a typical early adolescent, junior higher, *young teen.*

I ministered with students for about thirty years. In the early years especially, I was filled with advice for parents of teenagers—at church services, special seminars, personal counsel, and just about every opportunity. These days, however, I begin my seminars with the statement, "I used to be an expert on youth . . . until my eldest daughter entered junior high." Thinking back to my earlier parental advice, I may have had some pretty good material, but now I say those things with a lot more empathy. Because I have navigated two daughters through the rough waters of adolescence, I have become much more sensitive to what other parents are going through. I empathize with them because we have had the same experiences.

Junior high was traumatic for me because of all the horror stories one hears regarding those years. I was so fearful and finally came to the point where I asked the question: "Do I trust you, Lord?" He who began a good work within her, is he faithful to complete it? And the answer was yes.

Babs Swanson

Like all parents, Gail and I are amateurs, and yes, we made our share of mistakes in rearing Kara and Dana through the first ten or eleven years of life. But, on balance, we thought we had done fairly well . . . until the *button* got pushed.

I can't prove this, but I believe every child has a hidden button that gets pushed during the junior high or middle school years. Each child is unique, so some children go through this earlier and some later, but the transformation usually occurs around sixth or seventh grade. Until then, our girls were model children—well behaved, clean, even tempered, good, spiritual, and obedient. They weren't perfect, but as Garrison Keillor might say, "They were well above average." And we were so proud of them! Suddenly, however, without warning, almost overnight, they changed— they started acting different: unpredictable, defiant, and moody. Gail and I became insecure about our parenting ability. I can remember late-night discussions about Kara when we whispered the dreaded question to each other: "Are we creating a monster?" A few years later, we repeated the same experience with Dana. She was always our little hugger, sweet and compliant. We knew that *her* junior high experience would be different. But at thirteen, Dana's button got pushed, too, and we lost sleep again.

THE FEELINGS

We have seen our experience repeated by our friends and by parents of our kids' friends. During this fifth passage, when children approach the teenage years, parents probably feel more helpless and unsure of themselves than at any other time in their lives. Several men, fathers of junior highers in my neighborhood, asked my advice. These men weren't Christians and weren't especially conservative in their values or lifestyles, yet they were shocked at what they were seeing and hearing from their sons and daughters. Wanting to be good fathers, they looked for answers to these new and complex questions about parenting.

For many parents, the anxieties and fears come a year or two earlier. They've heard about the teenage years and have watched other people's kids struggle and rebel. These moms and dads are almost terrified with the notion that soon they will have a *teenager* in the house.

Darian Veerman says: *Although my two older children went through junior high successfully, approaching that time with our youngest, Bethany, is pretty scary. I'm really trying to help her find supportive, positive, and Christian friends.*

Remembering our own struggles during early adolescence, we fear for our children as they enter these turbulent years.

THE SYMPTOMS

The first symptoms of adolescence involve modern technology—the phone and the radio. Both are used constantly, often at the same time. Immediately upon entering his room, he turns on the stereo. As soon as she gets in the car, she turns on the radio and changes the station (and then continues to change stations after every song). One mother concluded that the phone had somehow become attached to her daughter's ear and would have to be surgically removed! Neither sex holds a monopoly on the telephone phenomenon—boys and girls alike can tie up the phone for hours at a time. They always have tons to talk about, usually involving "life-and-death" relationship issues.

Girls go through puberty like Grant took Richmond, alternating screaming laughter with screaming hysteria, interspersed with sullen silences when "she" (meaning me, her mother) comes into the room. Girls of 13 are already conscious of the fact that they have a figure and that it, like a really good lawn, will need life-long maintenance. They "diet" by skipping dinner and munch a lettuce leaf while the family gorges. They balance this with telling sympathetic friends over after-school pizza or French fries that "she" never serves anything but starches.

Janet Cool, "Nearing Adulthood, or: Why You'd Hate to Be 13 Again," Chicago Tribune, 24 January 1989, 1-13.

In junior high, Kara and her best friend seemed to do everything together. I remember driving Kara and the friend home after a full day of classes and basketball practice together. During the ride, they talked nonstop. I pulled up to the friend's house, and she got out of the car. What was Kara's parting line? That's right—"I'll call you."

Musical tastes arise as another source of misunderstanding and conflict. Almost without warning, these kids start listening to the rock stations, talking about their favorite artists, and buying albums. Along with this push into pop culture comes another phenomenon: the desire to see previously prohibited movies, videos, and TV shows. And each song, disc jockey, movie, video, and show can cause an argument, often ending with a defiant scream and a slamming door.

Conflicts concerning music and movies are not reserved for Christian homes. My non-Christian neighbors sought counsel because of problems in these areas. One man told me, "I can't believe what kids are seeing these days in the movies. I told Jenny that she can't go to any films rated PG-13, even if she is that age." Another expressed concern over the lyrics in his son's favorite songs.

Early adolescence also features enormous mood swings, that roller-coaster ride of emotions. No wonder parents are confused and frustrated during these years.

THE PROBLEMS
Besides the relationship stress and adolescent irritations, several other serious problems arise. First, there are continual conflicts at home. Junior highers seem to want to argue about everything. Privacy is a big deal. They will lock the bedroom door, write journals and notes, and talk in whispers on the phone. They don't want anyone, especially their parents, listening in. Violation of their space triggers arguments. So does any discussion of friendships or curfews or studying or church or extracurricular activities. These kids seem to challenge Mom and Dad on everything.

Another problem is the crisis in self-confidence. Early

adolescents want to be good at something, to feel competent. So they will take lessons, go out for teams, run for office, try out for plays, and so forth. When they fail, don't make the team, or lose, they may feel inferior, as though they are failures.

Doug Knox describes their family's experience with this part of the passage: *When Sara was in junior high, she wanted to try everything. Cheryl and I were happy for her to have the opportunity of new experiences, but at first, we wanted to protect her from the "agony of defeat." Then we realized that we shouldn't try to insulate Sara from failure because failures could motivate her to work harder, develop necessary skills, and help define who she is. Instead, we should be there to cheer and support Sara in her victories and defeats, successes and failures.*

Sixth, seventh, and eighth grades are the *crossroads years,* when kids begin to move in different directions. Most grade school children are good kids. Oh, there are a few bad ones, tough guys and troublemakers, but for the most part they still act like children. In junior high more definite social groupings form. Some are quite negative, including gangs. Kids begin to experiment with cigarettes, alcohol, drugs, and sex. Close friends part ways and new best friends are found. In elementary school a child plays with children in the neighborhood. But that changes in junior high, where relationships are forged through common interests, activities, and values. The former close friend may be in another social group. Friendship stresses and changes can be very painful for kids this age.

THE CAUSE

The underlying cause for all of the symptoms and problems can be summarized in one small word—*change*. Early adolescents experience change in every area of life: social, mental, spiritual, and physical.

Social

In addition to leaving behind old friends and finding new ones, junior highers are experimenting socially and trying to learn social skills. And they are beginning to be very conscious of the opposite sex, trying to determine who's *going out* with whom. Also, groups of friends become very important as these kids try to find a place to belong.

Friends mean everything. If you get the chance, listen to junior high conversations—most likely the topic will involve relationships: gossip, conflicts, and opposite-sex intrigues.

Early adolescents are changing socially.

Mental

Children think in black-and-white, concrete terms. Most adults are able to think conceptually. The change in thinking from concrete to conceptual (also known as formal operations) usually occurs during these years. Kids who haven't made this change may struggle in certain areas of study and feel left out of many classroom discussions.

Junior highers are experimenting with the ability to use abstract-reasoning skills. Some young people don't begin thinking conceptually until their sophomore year in high school. Do you remember taking geometry? Kids find that subject very easy or very difficult; there's no in-between. That's because it's different from any other class they have ever taken. Usually in math, a student's answers are either right or wrong. In geometry, however, *how* a student arrives at the answer can be more important than the answer itself. And there are all those theorems and proofs. Geometry involves thinking *conceptually*.

Early adolescents may begin to think that they're stupid because they don't understand what the teacher is talking about. Teachers may give more attention to students who understand and discuss ideas and concepts. Kids who are discovering these powers of the mind and their ability to think become family *lawyers*—they seem to argue about every little thing and can rationalize every action.

Junior highers are changing mentally.

Spiritual

Whether or not elementary school children go to church, it's no big deal to talk about church and God at school or on the playground. In junior high, however, religion isn't cool. That fact is learned quickly by junior highers, who are very sensitive to what their friends think and who want to be accepted by their peers.

Attendance at church activities will trigger many arguments with Mom and Dad. For example, junior high kids speak in extremes with their tendency to say, "Church is stupid!" or "Youth group is dumb!" Because these kids don't think conceptually yet, they may find that they don't understand the sermons or the Sunday school lessons. And because their friends are so important to them, they would rather be with their friends from school than the kids at church since most church youth groups draw from several different schools. To complicate things even more, many churches offer very little for this age group. They are too old for the traditional children's programs and too young for the youth group. No wonder junior high kids can easily become disenchanted with the whole church scene.

In addition, junior highers don't see much relevance of Bible stories and church to their lives. If they've grown up in church, they know the major Bible stories backwards and forwards. If they've been confirmed, they are familiar with important church doctrines. But it can all seem irrelevant to them. How do the Bible stories and church doctrines relate to the changes in their bodies? Their emotional ups and downs? Their fights with Mom and Dad? Their temptations to drink, smoke, and have sex? Young adolescents want answers but can't seem to find them in church.

Junior highers are changing spiritually.

Physical

Perhaps the most obvious changes during this time of life occur in the physical area. Adolescent bodies seem to change daily. Girls grow first and can feel like giants. Boys who grow late feel like shrimps and may never achieve the coveted roster spot on the football or basketball team. And junior highers can be clumsy as their feet and hands grow first, with the rest of body growth and coordination coming later. Growth spurts are common. (I grew a couple of inches and gained thirty pounds in one school year.) Kids this age can be very cruel to each other, mocking fellow students for being short, overweight, or unattractive, or for having other physical limitations.

———————————————————————————

To help get through the turbulence of adolescence, you should: (1) Keep the schedule simple. (2) Get plenty of rest. (3) Eat nutritious meals. (4) Stay on your knees.

Dr. James Dobson, Parenting Isn't for Cowards (Dallas: Word, 1987), p. 158.

———————————————————————————

Another dramatic physical change for early adolescents involves sex. Sex becomes a major obsession as raging hormones twist and turn their emotions. Suddenly boys become aware of girls and vice versa. The sexual organs begin to grow, and girls begin to menstruate. With all the new sexual awareness, talking gross, telling dirty jokes, acting tough, and swearing become common. And many kids begin to experiment with sex.

Early adolescents are changing physically.

As you can see, junior highers are coping with cataclysmic changes in every area of their lives. Researchers at Search Institute comment:

When looking at all the changes that occur during this period . . . one cannot help being struck with the sheer number of adaptations the young adolescent faces. No wonder there is turmoil. No wonder young adolescents sometimes seem overwhelmed and behave in ways that seem irrational to adults. They have a right to feel overwhelmed. There is a lot going on. (Peter Benson, Dorothy Williams, and Arthur Johnson, The Quicksilver Years, San Francisco: Harper & Row, 1987, p. 61)

HOW TO RESPOND

Although I have painted a dreary picture of the junior high/middle school years, there's a brighter side. In youth ministry I found these kids to be a lot of fun and very rewarding to work with—although I still struggled when my own kids were this age. If youth ministers and parents don't get *psyched out* but work hard to relate, they will have many opportunities to teach and develop godly character. Here's what you can do.

1. Understand

The phrase "To know all is to forgive all" contains a profound and practical truth. If I know a person and what they are going through, I will be more understanding and forgiving of that person.

Ted has had a bad day. It started at 6:30 A.M. when he cut himself shaving. Next, he spilled coffee on his shirt as he was rushing out the door, trying to sip on his way to the car. By running late, he hit the height of the morning rush hour and was late for a meeting at the office where he was supposed to make a presentation, thus aggravating his boss. Later, he learned that an important deal fell through. To top it off, on the way home he was stopped by a state trooper. As he stumbles through the door at 7:00 P.M., he is greeted by his wife, Amber, who says tersely, "Why are you late? Dinner's cold." When Ted mumbles a gruff reply, Amber raises her voice and retorts: "You're always such a grouch when you come home. Don't take it out on me—I've had a rough day, too!" Ted puts down his briefcase and slumps into his chair at the table, thinking, *If you only knew what I've been through today, you would understand.*

Amber is thinking much the same thing. Her day hasn't been a piece of cake either. In fact, she has had to deal with a sick child, a stopped-up toilet, a complication in the small business she runs out of the house, and a persistent sales representative. Often Amber has wanted to scream in frustration and anger. She knows that her remarks to Ted weren't very loving, but she thinks, *If only you knew what I've been through today, you would understand.*

Knowing what a person has been through doesn't excuse *all* of their behavior. A person is responsible for their actions—we shouldn't acquit a murderer, for example, just because he had a bad childhood. But it does help us to be much more understanding and able to solve root problems.

I think most adults would be more forgiving of early adolescents if they knew what these kids were feeling and encountering every day. Remember, they are *rushed.* In this age of information, they already know more about drugs, crime, missing kids, terrorism, abuse, and wars than their parents knew five years after high school. Their schedules are packed with activities, and many young teens have serious stress fractures in their emotions.

Remember also that junior highers are *pressured and tempted:* to drink, to be sexually active, and to do a host of other things that they know are wrong. The teachers and politicians may preach Just Say No, but the movies, musicians, disc jockeys, and videos all shout, "Just say yes."

Finally, remember that these kids are *growing and changing.* These changes wreak havoc with junior highers' emotions and can lead to a variety of uncharacteristic attitudes and behaviors.

Thus, if you really understand what early adolescents are going through, you will be much more forgiving and able to deal with your junior higher's real needs and problems.

2. Communicate

The second positive action you can take is to communicate with your early adolescent child. Tom and Julie Essenburg took a proactive approach to communication with their son, Ben: *In our first conflicts with Ben during junior high, we explained that Mom and Dad had never been parents of a teenager before and that we all needed to learn together. We needed to work at forgiving and being forgiven, and we had to work at keeping the lines of communication open.*

Attitude

Communication begins with *attitude*—you should choose a

positive attitude. Too many adults make fun of junior highers and belittle their styles, physical characteristics, musical tastes, friends, and so forth. But that only leads to confrontation and alienation. Instead, hold your tongue whenever you are tempted to snap back with caustic, cutting, or sarcastic comments. Remember the teaching of Ephesians 6:4: "Fathers, do not exasperate your children; instead, bring them up in the training and instruction of the Lord" (NIV).

A positive attitude also means carefully choosing your battles. Every day you will find many issues about which to argue and fight. But if you're honest, you would have to admit that most of the issues really aren't very important. Is Jason's room a mess? Instead of nagging him to clean it, shut the door so you won't see it. Does Danielle slouch in the family room and try to study with her music on? Let it go—if her grades don't suffer, what's the difference? Some parents use up all their ammunition in the little skirmishes. Then when something serious happens, they have no reserves left for the major battles.

A positive attitude will lead to positive communication.

Listening

Communication also involves *listening*. Listen with your *eyes* as well as your ears. Look for clues in your son's or daughter's body language. If she has been hurt by a friend's gossip, she will show it in the way she walks around the house. He may be brooding because he is depressed about his height . . . or anxious about basketball tryouts . . . or angry at someone who's been picking on him at school.

When junior highers talk, you should listen—*really listen,* not just look at them, waiting for your chance to speak while thinking of what you will say. And listening means taking seriously what your teen tells you.

I remember a seventh grade romance. During a week of summer camp, I fell hopelessly in love with a girl from another church in a city many miles away from me. When I left her, I thought my heart would break. But when I told my youth director about my feelings, he laughed and said, "Oh, that'll last about ten letters and two phone calls." He was right, of course, but he was wrong in saying it. At the time, I was hurt by his flippant attitude—and I still remember the incident.

You will learn much simply by being quiet and listening to your child talk. This works especially well as you are driving your child and their friends somewhere. They will talk nonstop as though you are invisible, and they will cover the whole range of topics, from who's going out with whom to what happened in school that day. If you try to enter the conversation, however, they will become very quiet and return to the typical one-word answers.

Another important aspect of listening is choosing the right time to talk. When Kara was in seventh grade, at times she would make outrageous statements at the dinner table. For example, she might describe a friend getting into trouble at school, talk about an R-rated video, or state how much she hated a certain teacher. My natural reaction was to respond immediately, pointing out the error of her friend's ways, pontificating about our family's video-watching standards, or arguing with her about the importance of doing one's best in school. Each time I did that, it was a disaster. Kara would become defensive about her friend, the video, or whatever, and become angry with me. I had to learn to listen quietly (that's tough for me) and let Kara talk it all out. Then, later in the evening when I was helping her with homework or just before bed, often I would broach the controversial subject with her. Usually she would be much less defensive and more open to talk. For example, I might say, "At dinner you told us about what Cyndi did at school. What do you think about what she did?" Then Kara would honestly express her feelings, and I would be able to talk about why I thought her friend's behavior was not acceptable. The same would be true for a discussion of the forbidden video or any other topic. The teachable moments usually came later in the evening when we had all settled back into a more relaxed family routine.

Learn to be a good listener.

We find that young people want to talk to their parents about issues that interest them, puzzle them, trouble them and that parents want to talk with their children. But, in most instances, the conversations never happen.

To be sure, some talking takes place, but only in some families, and, even for them, not often enough, or for long enough. Too often, household routines, school schedules, the family's comings and goings, and television's mesmerizing distractions carry parents and children along, week after week, until suddenly the children are graduating from high school, and all the things they meant some day to talk about—and the right times to do it—have vanished.

Peter Benson, Dorothy Williams, and Arthur Johnson, The Quicksilver Years (San Francisco: Harper & Row, 1987), p. 212.

Vocabulary

Effective communication also means using words that your child understands. I'm not referring to teenage clichés or slang—you shouldn't try to talk like a teenager again. But you should think carefully about your audience and their ability to concentrate and understand.

A few years ago I was coaching a sixth and seventh grade girls basketball team. During one practice, my fellow coaches and I were teaching how to play zone defense. After demonstrating what happens when an offensive player leaves a certain zone, one of the coaches said, "If the girl leaves your zone, you don't have to worry about her. The onus is on the player over here." I almost laughed out loud as I looked at the puzzled expressions on the girls' faces. *Onus? What's an onus?* they thought as they checked their clothes to see if they had any on them already.

If you want to get through to your junior high kid, you should keep the vocabulary simple and concrete, and ask for feedback to see if they really understand what you are trying to explain.

This also applies to rules and discipline. It is important to carefully and clearly explain your rules, the parameters of behavior, and the consequences of violating them. Some parents put the rules in writing so there will be no misunderstanding. Obviously, we can't think of every possible circumstance and potential infraction, but important areas such as schoolwork, church, curfew, chores, and respect for others should be covered.

Take time to talk things through. Don't just dismiss your child summarily, exerting your authority. According to a number of adults surveyed by Greg Johnson and Mike Yorkey, the least effective ways of resolving conflicts included these statements by parents:

- ◆ "I'm the parent."
- ◆ "Because I told you so."
- ◆ "When your dad gets home, . . ."
- ◆ "I don't have energy for this."
- ◆ "Don't sass me."
- ◆ "Go to your room."

Also, children *hated* being yelled at—this was the most common response. Others heard ultimatums every hour, and the threats lost their impact (*Faithful Parents, Faithful Kids.* Wheaton, Ill.: Tyndale House, 1993, pp. 26–27).

Take time to talk through the issues, and communicate in language your adolescent understands.

Teachable Moments

Great opportunities for positive communication occur almost daily with junior highers. But you need to be sensitive to the teachable moments and take advantage of them when they occur—solving a specific problem, sharing from your experience and wisdom, pointing to a relevant biblical text, and praying together. Tom Essenburg says that one of the benefits of his son learning to think conceptually is that they can talk about the consequences of certain actions. "Through these years, I've become more of a friend to Ben than just his parent."

Larry Kreider tells of an experience that his son had when he was twelve years old: *Brett took the bus to school. Each morning at least twenty-five kids would gather at the bus stop. That morning we sent Brett off to school, thinking everything was fine. But about forty-five minutes later, we received a call from the police saying that they had my son in their custody. At the bus stop there was a traffic counter, the kind with the rubber hose that stretches across the street. Some of the kids waiting for the bus thought they would have a little fun and started jumping up and down on the rubber hose, causing the numbers to go up on the counter. Brett was already on the bus when the police showed up. They asked one of the kids if anyone else had been jumping on the hose, and he said, "Yes, Brett was." So they took him off the bus, put him in the back of the police car, and took him to the station.*

I was upset because it seemed like overkill by the police. But I was also aware that Brett had been influenced by his peers to do something that was wrong. I had a real struggle to help him understand and respect the authority of the police while helping him see that he shouldn't have joined in the jumping. I told Brett that we have to live by the rules and obey the law and that what he did was not right. I also explained that I thought the police were wrong, too. It became a wonderful opportunity to teach Brett about our responsibility to respect the law, even in a difficult situation.

Your teachable moments may not be as obvious, but you will have them. Look for them.

Because early adolescents are focused on *competence,* this is the ideal time to teach them skills. We model values, but we have to teach skills. A skill begins with the words *how to.* Good coaches spend hours teaching their players the basic skills of the game: how to kick a soccer ball, how to pitch, how to serve, how to shoot a free throw, and so forth.

Beyond the athletic field, junior highers need to learn skills that will help them win in the game of life. These important life skills include how to study, how to get along with the opposite sex, how to talk to an adult, how to be a good friend, how to solve problems, and how to handle money, just to name a few. Spiritual life skills should also be taught: how to pray, how to study the Bible, how to worship, how to explain what you believe, and others. Early adolescents are eager to learn *how to* do almost anything, and you can tap into that motivation by teaching your child life skills. Although they may look and sound disinterested, children look to their parents to teach them practical skills for living as an adult.

Model values, teach skills, and watch for teachable moments.

Communication is very important at this age. But communication goes both ways and begins with a positive attitude and active listening on your part. It also involves speaking clearly in language your child understands and looking for those special teachable moments.

3. Love

The third positive action you can take is to *love*. As defined by our culture, love usually is described as a noun. It is something a person finds, falls into, has, and feels. But in Scripture, love is an attitude and a verb—it involves a choice to act on someone's behalf. John 3:16 states: "For God so loved the world that he gave. . . ." Christ's love for us sent him to the cross. And 1 Corinthians 13 is packed with loving attitudes and actions. So how can you show love to junior highers? By choosing to act in love toward them, even when they aren't very lovable and even when they irritate and frustrate you.

Stay Close

Some parents assume that adolescents are becoming independent and don't want them around. So these parents begin to withdraw emotionally and physically from their kids during sixth, seventh, and eighth grades. But studies have shown that early adolescents want a close family and still enjoy having Mom and Dad involved in their lives.

When I was putting together the junior high ministry

team for the church I attend, I looked for parents of kids in the group who were willing to participate. I have found that my involvement with my girls when they were in junior high enhanced my relationship with them—they were proud of me, and we drew closer. And I thoroughly enjoyed coaching soccer, basketball, and softball, helping with the church youth group, teaching Sunday school, and running Campus Life/JV at their middle school. I never got the feeling that Kara or Dana thought I was cramping their style or inhibiting their social lives.

Though some kids genuinely resent their parents' involvement, they are the exception, not the rule. Unfortunately, many parents take the emotional comments and quick reactions of their early adolescents literally. For example, Scott might say, "I don't want to go to youth group. It's stupid and boring!" Not wanting to push Scott and afraid that they might turn him off to church altogether, Scott's parents give in and allow him to stay home. Instead, if they have confidence in the junior high ministry team, they probably should insist that Scott go to the youth group, trusting that he will have a good time there and may even learn something. When I would meet with the parents of the junior highers at church, I would urge them to bring their kids to our activities, even over their protests, and trust us to minister effectively with them. Almost without exception, the most vocal junior high objectors would settle into the group and have a great time—once they got there.

The principle holds true for parental involvement. Some parents might argue, "It's easy for you to coach your daughter and to work with her youth group, Dave, because you have a lot of experience in junior high ministry." But having experience or being cool has very little to do with it. I have seen parents who would be the most unlikely candidates for youth ministry become involved and minister effectively *with their own kids in the group.* When asked if he would want Mom and Dad teaching his Sunday school class, Scott might respond, "Are you kidding? Of course not!" I submit, however, that Scott would get used to the idea and eventually enjoy having his parents involved. The junior high ministry team at my church is composed almost entirely of parents of kids in the group, and the involvement of those parents has improved their relationship with their kids. Don't be intimidated by what you *think* your junior high child might feel about you being there or by their comments. Look for ways to get involved—don't withdraw.

Loving means looking for positive and fun ways to stay involved with your child.

Clear the Schedule

Loving also means clearing your schedule so that you will have time and emotional energy to spend with your child. If you are never at home, you probably won't be there when *teachable moments* and nuggets of *quality time* arise. If you're extremely busy at work, in the community, or at church, you won't have time or energy to teach your children anything. Learn to say no to many of your other commitments so that you can spend time with your child.

Affirm

Another aspect of love is affirmation. It is easy for junior highers to feel as though they can't do anything right. They hear a continual barrage of criticism and correction (most of it deserved) from parents, bus drivers, teachers, study-hall monitors, coaches, neighbors, and friends. So it's up to you to give positive feedback. This means trying to catch your child doing something *good* and *right,* and then praising them for it.

This is especially important in the area of competence. If you have taught your son how to make cookies or lasagna, praise your chef for what he did right and don't point out the imperfections in the final product. If you watch your daughter's seventh grade volleyball game, look for actions and incidents to affirm: her enthusiasm on the bench, quick footwork, encouragement of other team members, or one serve that made it over the net.

In his counseling practice, Kirby Hanawalt observed what happens when parents hold unrealistic expectations and then continually emphasize the negative. He relates the following incident: *"She is so beautiful and has so much potential. We wanted to give her every chance that we could. We have had her in gymnastics, acting, and private school. How could she do this to us?"*

Cindy's parents talked as if she were not in the room. They belittled her, telling me how she had become a tramp and that they wouldn't be surprised if she were on drugs. They wondered if she could have been another person's child—had someone switched children at birth?

Cindy had been the ideal child until she was fourteen years of age. She had led her friends to the Lord, and she had been well mannered, active in sports, and a straight-A student. She had been living up to her parents' every desire.

I asked the parents to leave the room, and I asked a simple question: "What does it feel like to always have to live up to your parents' expectations?" Cindy's eyes filled with tears as she opened up and told me how difficult it was to please them. The more she tried, the more they wanted. Finally, she had come to realize that she could no longer live like that. Drugs and sex for money had no expectations or demands. Besides, they killed the pain of always having to live to please others.

When parents' desires and dreams for their child get in the way of the child's own hopes, I find the *blueprint for disaster*. Here's how to guarantee trouble.

1. Demand that your child does what you want, never listening to their input.
2. Tell your child how they must act and what they will be, because you, the parent, knows what is best.
3. When your child fails, point out why they need you so much.
4. Never give a compliment for anything your child does.

Kirby Hanawalt, a marriage and family counselor for Greater Vancouver (Canada) Youth for Christ.

Cindy needed to get away from the pressure, to find other outlets to prove her competence, and, most of all, to be affirmed!

Love means letting your kid know that you think they are special and good.

Discipline

A final but crucial way to show love for your early adolescent is to discipline them. No matter how much your young teen pushes against the limits, whines, argues, debates, and rationalizes, they *need and want the limits.* In fact, without rules, guidelines, punishments, and rewards, early adolescents feel very insecure.

A few years ago, I was driving Kara and a friend to a basketball game. I listened as they talked nonstop in the backseat. When they began talking about teachers and school, something the friend said caught my ear. In describing a certain teacher, she said, "He's not a good teacher. He lets us get away with anything." Kara's friend was expressing what most early adolescents feel—they really want someone to set limits, to tell them "No! Stop!" or "That's not acceptable!" and to maintain order.

Some parents are afraid to exercise discipline with their children at this age. Fearful of alienating them or just intimidated by the child's aggressive arguments, these parents give in and let their kids get away with anything. Instead, carefully and clearly explain the rules, and then calmly and lovingly enforce them. Proverbs 15:1 gives invaluable counsel for this: "A gentle answer turns away wrath, but a harsh word stirs up anger" (NIV). Firm enforcement of the rules does not mean loud and angry—gentleness will be much more effective.

By the way, one of the most often used junior high arguments is that other parents let *their* kids go to R-rated movies, hang out at the mall, watch the popular television show, wear the revealing clothes, go to the party, and do other questionable activities. I have found, however, that each of these *other* parents may, in fact, be more permissive than Gail and I in a specific area, but may also be more strict in others. Many of them are hearing the same arguments from their kids, who may be using *us* as ammunition.

Art Wittmann tells about an experience he had with his oldest daughter, Heather, when she was in sixth grade: *Heather wanted to go to a boy-girl party. Carol and I talked it over and weren't sure what to do. I took Heather aside to have a father-to-daughter talk. I explained that as the oldest child, she was blazing new territory for us as parents. I also tried to explain the difference between liberal and conservative and that we were on the conservative side. At this point in the discussion, Heather could see where I was headed and was not happy. Finally, with fear and trembling, I took a firm stand and said, "You are not going to go."*

A few days later, Carol was talking with a neighbor whose son was the same age as Heather and had also been invited to the party. In the course of the conversation the neighbor remarked, "I am so glad you told Heather she couldn't go. That made it much easier for us to say no as well."

Regardless of what other parents do, we have the God-given responsibility to rear *our* children, not theirs, so we shouldn't worry about what other junior highers are or are not allowed to do. Often we will find, as Art did, that other parents feel the same way we do but don't have the courage to be firm and make the right decision.

Mark Senter tells about the time that he and Ruth decided to take the kids to see a movie that had received good reviews and was recommended for the whole family. Jori was in sixth grade at the time, and Nick was in elementary school. About forty minutes into it, there was a questionable scene. Ruth poked Mark in the ribs and suggested that they leave. Mark whispered back that he was sure this was an isolated incident and that they should wait it out. About ten minutes later, however, there was another very suggestive scene. Not waiting for Ruth's urging this time, Mark gathered the family and they left the packed theater. Jori was visibly upset and asked why. Mark replied that he would tell her later. As they were exiting, however, Mark noticed that many of Jori's friends were waiting in the lobby for the next showing. They greeted her and asked about the movie (probably wondering why the family was leaving so early). In the car Jori expressed her anger at the situation, asked why they had to leave, and blasted Mom and Dad. As they pulled into the driveway, Mark sent Jori to her room. Off she stomped, yelling, "I never want to go with you, ever again!"

As Mark thought about the situation, he suddenly realized the cause for Jori's outburst. It wasn't really about the movie but about being embarrassed in front of her friends. Jori knew that she would have to face those kids at school on Monday, and they would undoubtedly ask about the incident. What could she possibly say?

Mark went to Jori's room and tried to calm her down. Then he explained his actions and apologized for embarrassing her. He said, "I'm sorry that you were embarrassed. I don't ever want to embarrass you again, but we took that risk. Please forgive us for that, but realize that Mom and I were doing what we had to do." That opened the door to a very important conversation.

About six months later, Jori went to a movie with a friend. Mark dropped them off and drove home. About ten minutes later, Jori called and asked him to pick her up. In the car she explained that it was the worst movie she had ever seen, so she had walked out and had even asked the theater manager for her money back. Then she added, "Dad, if we hadn't walked out six months ago, I wouldn't have had the courage to do it today."

Although it was an unpleasant experience, Mark and Ruth's determination to model their values and enforce their rules paid off in Jori's life. Early adolescents need limits—your child wants you to set them and enforce them.

Remember, too, that *discipline* is more than punishment; it is positive action to direct behavior. Our goal as parents should be to teach our children to become self-disciplined so that they will do what is right when they have moved beyond our surveillance and rule enforcement. Dr. Kevin Lehman, a psychologist and best-selling author, has written much about *reality discipline,* allowing children to experience the natural results of their actions whenever possible. For example, Mom has told the kids about caring for their clothes, hanging them up, folding them and putting them away, or putting them in the laundry hamper to be washed. Instead of picking up after the kids and nagging them about their behavior, she allows them to throw the clothes in a pile in their rooms. Then she allows them to not have any clean or pressed clothes to wear. The kids learn that their actions have consequences, so they decide to take care of their clothes.

Gail and I tried this successfully with both girls regarding getting up in the morning. It would have been easy for us to wake them up every day, but they wouldn't have learned to be self-disciplined in this area. So when Kara was in the sixth grade, we bought her an alarm clock, told her how to work it, and explained that she had to get up right away when it went off. The first couple of times, she slept through. We woke her and reminded her of the importance of getting up on her own, and we explained that now she would be totally on her own. The next day she slept through the alarm again. Half an hour later she awoke, looked at the clock, panicked, and rushed to get ready for school. From that point on she got out of bed as soon as the alarm sounded.

It's never too early to begin teaching children that their actions have consequences. Obviously you have to be sensitive to the age of the child and keep them from harm. For example, don't teach a toddler a *lesson* by allowing him to touch a hot stove. But children need to become self-disciplined. Junior high is a great time to use reality discipline. (For more on this, see Dr. Lehman's book, *Making Children Mind without Losing Yours,* Old Tappan, N.J.: Revell, 1984.)

Early adolescents need and want limits, and they need to learn to be self-disciplined.

Parenting a teen can be a difficult passage—a roller-coaster ride that never seems to end. But it does. And you can even enjoy the ride if you *understand, communicate,* and *love.*

LET'S THINK ABOUT IT

Warnings

◆ *Don't withdraw from your junior high kids.* They still want and need your involvement in their lives. Open your schedule and work at spending time with them.

◆ *Don't argue and fight over every little thing.* Choose your battles carefully.

◆ *Don't overreact and lose your cool.* Kids won't listen when you're yelling and handing out totally unrealistic punishments (for example, "You're grounded for life!"). Instead, calmly explain your position and be firm in your enforcement of your rules.

◆ *Don't take what they say as literal truth.* Junior highers will tend to speak in extremes (everything is "great" or "stupid," "Everybody's doing it," "The teacher hates me," "All the other kids' parents let them," etc.). Talk to the teacher, coach, church youth leader, and other parents before making judgments.

Opportunities

◆ *Look for teachable moments* to communicate values and

develop skills. Conflicts with friends, questions about church, physical changes, struggles and pressures at school, and many other situations can provide excellent opportunities to reinforce biblical values and teach life skills.

- *Get involved with your child.* Junior highers respect adult authority, and most don't mind being with their parents.

- *Open your home to your child's friends.* Let your home be the place where kids feel accepted and where they have fun.

- *Help your young adolescent become self-disciplined.* Use reality discipline to guide them toward this goal.

- *Pray for your junior higher.* They are going through very important changes in life.

- *Reach out to other parents who are struggling with their early adolescents.* This is a great time to build relationships, support each other, and share the gospel.

Lessons

- *Early adolescence isn't fatal.* There's light at the end of this passage as kids grow through the changes and move toward maturity.

- *Rules and discipline are important.* Junior highers have trouble controlling themselves—they need and want limits (see Proverbs 13:24).

- *Kids this age need to learn spiritual life skills.* Encourage your church to develop and deepen the junior high ministry, emphasizing interesting, relevant, and fun activities.

+ *You aren't raising a monster.* Your child is normal, and most parents of early adolescents are experiencing the same questions and struggles (see 1 Corinthians 10:13).

Resources

+ *The McGee and Me! series* (produced by Focus on the Family and Tyndale House Publishers) are outstanding Christian videos that entertain and teach. Episodes one through nine are appreciated most by elementary school children, but the New Adventures, episodes ten through twelve, are geared to junior highers. Also available is *McGee and Me! The Special Event for Kids,* a creative six-session curriculum that uses the first five videos in the series—ideal for Sunday school, vacation Bible school, and neighborhood outreach.

+ *Breakaway* and *Brio* are magazines published by Focus on the Family. Written specifically for junior high students, each issue is loaded with stories, columns, cartoons, and other features designed to inspire, instruct, and entertain. For more information, write to Focus on the Family, P.O. Box 35500, Colorado Springs, CO 80935-3550, or call 719-531-3400.

+ *Campus Life/JV* is the junior high ministry of Youth for Christ/USA. They have three manuals of meetings that center on teaching kids life skills. To purchase the manuals or for more information on the Campus Life/JV ministry, write to Youth for Christ/USA at P.O.

Box 228822, Denver, CO 80222, or call 303-843-9000.

* *Choice Adventures* is a series of books for early adolescents. Published by Tyndale House, these exciting stories center around the adventures of a group of junior highers in a small town outside of Washington, D.C. Each book contains a number of different story lines that the reader chooses by making choices in the story. The stories emphasize Christian values and the consequences of making certain choices in life. The first book in this series, *The Mysterious Old Church,* was written by Neil Wilson and was published in 1991.

* *Life Application Bible for Students* (Wheaton, Ill.: Tyndale House, 1992). This edition of the Bible was written especially for junior high and early high school students. Available in *The Living Bible* and the New King James Version, the Bible contains hundreds of notes that help the young person understand the Bible and apply it to their life. The features include Moral Dilemma notes, Personality Profiles, Ultimate Issue notes, Life-Changer Index, "I Wonder" notes, "Where to Find It" Index, Life Application notes, highlighted memory verses, a Bible reading plan, a follow-through course for new Christians, "Here's What I Did" notes, and much more.

* *Ready for Life* (Wheaton, Ill.: Victor, 1994). This is a collection of six books, each with six lessons for junior highers. Written for use in Sunday school classes, youth group meetings, seminars, retreats, or camps, these les-

sons center around teaching life skills. Parents can easily adapt the material for use at home.

- *Sticky Situations* is a board game from Tyndale House and Focus on the Family featuring McGee from *McGee and Me!* When players land on a Sticky Situation square, they read a card that describes a situation in which a moral or ethical decision must be made. Consequences follow each decision (determined by a roll of the die). The game is fun, interesting, and instructive.

- David R. Veerman, *Reaching Kids before High School* (Wheaton, Ill.: Victor, 1990). In this book I describe the junior high experience and explain how to minister effectively to this age group. Youth workers and parents have found it to be helpful.

Driving Us Crazy

———————

6

Remember, Miss Anderson, we at B-1 Driving School are professionals. There's no need to be nervous. Remember our motto: You can B-1, too. That was, uh, just a little joke.

That's good—you put your seat belt on, started the car, checked the rearview mirror, and made sure the radio, windshield wipers, and turn signals all work. But, uh, you might want to close the door before pulling out.

You're doing fine now. Just a little faster would be OK. Uh, don't worry about the honking—just push down a little bit more and ease up and beyond fifteen miles per hour. Yes, maybe it would be good to get off the expressway. Get off at the next exit. No! Not here! I meant the next exit—two miles down the road. But you made it. By the way, it's always good to be in the right-hand lane when you exit right. . . . You don't think those other drivers minded that you cut them off like that? Uh, Miss Anderson, they weren't waving at you; they were . . . never mind.

OK, now we're coming to a red light, so slow down. No—take your foot off the gas pedal and put it on the brake pedal. . . . Not so hard! That's all right—I had my shoulder harness in place, and I'll recover in a couple of months from the whiplash.

The light is green so you can go now. . . . I know that light is red, but your light is green, so pull ahead—don't mind the honking behind us.

Now that was a beautiful right turn, Miss Anderson— probably one of the best turns I've seen in a long time. . . . You're welcome. . . . But we're on a one-way street! . . . Yes, I know you're only going one way, but it's the wrong way. Do you notice all those cars coming at us and swerving? . . . Wait—why are you backing up so fast? . . . You want to go the right way?

Whoa! How did you do that? A quick 180-degree turn? Oh, you saw it on TV. Hmmm. Well, at least we're going the right direction.

What does a flashing light mean? Well, if it's a flashing

*yellow light, it means caution, and a flashing red means
. . . wait a minute, where did you see one? In the rearview
mirror . . . on top of the blue-and-white car . . . I see. No,
wait, it doesn't mean step on the gas. . . . I don't care if you
did see it on TV. . . .*

Driving and driver's training has made great material for
comedians for several decades. We laugh because we identify
with the student and imagine what the instructor must be
feeling and because we've been at the mercy of less-than-com-
petent drivers. But it's no laughing matter when we picture
our teenager behind the wheel. That's a different story.

The sobering vision for parents is more like this: A vehicle
costing thousands of dollars and weighing thousands of
pounds, powered by internal explosions and guided by an
inexperienced adolescent, is hurtling headlong at incredible
speeds down rain- and snow-slicked highways in the company of other drivers—many of whom may be incompetent,
irresponsible, or under the influence of alcohol or drugs. It's
not a pretty picture and certainly not funny.

Yet our teens eagerly anticipate receiving the coveted driver's license and the opportunity to drive the family car. We
know it has to happen sooner or later, so with great ambivalence and even fear, we give in and sign them up for driver's
ed . . . and we head through this sixth passage of parenting.

A RITE OF PASSAGE
Kids push for the right to drive because driving has become
a symbol of their emergence into the adult world. In prim-

itive societies, this rite of passage might involve surviving overnight in the jungle, tracking and killing a specified wild animal, climbing a mountain, or attaining proficiency in the use of a weapon, horse, or canoe. Today, getting the license and driving means that the child no longer is a child and has grown up, especially in the eyes of peers. Driving means independence and freedom.

Make no mistake, for most kids this is very serious business. I knew that typically *boys* loved cars and driving, but I didn't know girls shared that enthusiasm. So I was unprepared for the intensity of my daughters' desire to drive. Because taking driver's education in school would have postponed the event a few months, Kara and many of her friends insisted on having private lessons so they could get their licenses *on* their sixteenth birthday. Dana turned fifteen while I was writing this book and already was lobbying to take driving lessons six months before her sixteenth birthday.

Parenthood can be difficult, but it also has its rewards. In the end, there's no substitute for the sense of satisfaction that comes from watching as your children, under your steady guiding hand, develop from tiny, helpless Frequent Barfer modules into full-grown, self-reliant young adults fully capable of crashing your car into a day-care center.

Dave Barry

This significant milestone for kids is also a passage for their parents as they encounter emotions and conflicts associated with the event. As with the other parenting passages, Gail and I were surprised by our feelings as Kara pressured and pushed to be able to drive. Of course, we knew our insurance premiums would increase dramatically and we would incur other related expenses. But those didn't bother us nearly as much as the idea of our little girl actually driving a car.

I believe that parents struggle during this passage for three main reasons.

MEMORIES

The first reason for our negative feelings at this passage is the clear memory of our own early driving experiences. We remember reckless moments, irresponsible acts, and near tragedies. Thinking back to my high school days, I'm amazed at the freedom my parents gave me with the car. One Saturday my friends and I drove a couple of hours away to visit girls we had met at church camp earlier in the summer. I can remember fighting sleep on the drive. Instead of stopping to rest or get a cup of coffee, I was determined to gut it out. I faded in and out as I drove with my companions sound asleep beside me, but somehow, by God's grace, I made it safely home. I also remember showing off and popping the clutch as I tried to beat the car next to me off the line at the stoplight. Most parents remember similar incidents, from overloading the car with friends to running a stop sign and narrowly missing a car in the intersection. They know, from personal experience, how kids drive.

Perhaps the most vivid memory with cars involves dating. When I was growing up, *parking* didn't refer to a skill learned in driver's education class. Besides providing quick and convenient transportation to and from the date itself, a car could become a private, intimate place for a variety of romantic activities. We parents remember finding Campground Road, the quarry, McDowell Forest Preserve, Lake Avenue, Alpine Park, and an assortment of country lanes and dead-end streets. Usually we don't talk about those experiences because we still feel guilty and ashamed about many of the things we did. Unlike the fogged-up car windows, our memories are clear, and we don't want our kids to repeat our mistakes.

CONCERN

Second, parents don't like the idea of their children driving cars because of genuine concerns for safety. Insurance companies increase their rates for good reason—the negative statistics for young drivers. Whether it's the feeling of power, the exhilaration of speed, the urge to show off, or the lack of skill, teenagers tend to drive more recklessly than others. In my neighborhood, on the highway, and in the high school parking lot, daily I see kids driving well beyond safe limits.

One reason for this carelessness is the youthful feeling of immortality—that nothing bad can happen to them, especially in a car where they are surrounded by protective metal, glass, plastic, and fiberglass. And they feel as though they are in control. It's a false security, of course, but that is how most drivers, especially young ones, feel.

Myrllis Aycock says: *When Craig got his driver's license, I was*

148

scared. This kid is adventurous. On snowy, icy days when I picked him up from school, he'd ask me to let him drive home. "Mom, I need to learn to drive on ice and snow also." So I moved over and let him drive—braking in the passenger seat all the way home!

Another genuine cause for parental concern is other drivers on the road. It seems as though every day we read tragic reports of someone losing control and swerving into oncoming lanes, killing themselves and the occupants of another vehicle. We even hear of violent altercations over minor incidents in traffic. And drunk drivers continue to plague us. Driving instructors teach *defensive driving*—being aware of other cars and assuming the worst of other drivers. But even defensive drivers can become victims when other drivers use drugs or alcohol. And teenagers tend to take the *offensive* in the way they drive, and they are easily distracted by friends and the radio or tape player.

One thing I have realized is that God doesn't give me the grace to handle things that my children face in their world. I am horrified with what they have to confront daily, but it is not me who has to deal with the issues. It's them. God is powerful in their lives, showing them ways out of temptation, giving them confidence in him and the ability to cope in a wicked world.

Babs Swanson

Driver safety also enters the family discussion through another door during these years—the issue of *riding* in a car driven by another teenager. Frank won't be sixteen until March, so he can't drive until then. But Gregg just got his license and will be driving to school from now on. Frank asks if he can ride to and from school with Gregg, his neighbor and friend. The tension is heightened because the only realistic alternative for Frank is to continue riding the bus. Frank and most of his friends think the school bus is for little kids and they are beyond that. Mom and Dad don't appreciate that line of thinking. After all, their tax dollars pay for the bus transportation, and the bus stop is convenient, only two houses away. And they point out that the bus and Gregg's car would get to school at about the same time. Also, although they like Gregg, they don't think he is very responsible—he is always saying and doing goofy things. They can't imagine what he might do behind the wheel. So an argument ensues as Frank's parents tell him that he can't ride with Gregg until Gregg has had more experience as a driver.

Our concerns for safety are rooted in reality.

SYMBOL

Third, parents face anxious feelings during this passage because the driver's license is another indication that our children are growing up and away from us. The automobile, a marvelous invention, revolutionized personal transportation. It also revolutionized the social scene. Before cars (B.C.), when the porch swing stopped creaking, an alert mom could bring lemonade out to the "swinging" couple. Today, in a matter of minutes, the boy and girl can be miles away from Mom, Dad, and any other potential chaperones.

Teens without cars are dependent on others and are limited in where they can go and what they can do. With a car they can come and go as they please . . . to the game, to a movie, or to a friend's house . . . (or can say that they're going to the game and go to a friend's house instead). With a car teenagers have *freedom.*

The driver's license is a symbol of independence. We know, of course, that eventually our children must leave home and live on their own, apart from us. That's what it means to grow up. When an adult still acts like a young child and depends totally on his parents for food, shelter, and emotional support, something is not right. We certainly don't want that for our children, but it's tough to let go. Yet it seems as though that's what we have been doing ever since the fourth passage when we sent them off to school.

THE PUSH FOR INDEPENDENCE

During this time of life, we see other signs of their growing push for independence.

1. *They insist on privacy* and may even become very secretive. Those who have a room of their own will keep the door shut, even when they're gone. In addition, they are outraged if we happen to overhear a phone conversation or accidentally read a note from a friend or a journal entry. And they

may not willingly divulge personal information to us, even about homework.

Up through junior high, Kara brought her papers and tests home, so Gail and I knew how she was doing. At times she asked us for help with homework assignments, and we quizzed her in preparation for big tests. In high school, however, we always had to ask about school; then Kara would take offense and react as though we were prying. We explained our motives and warned Kara that her grades had better not suffer. Kara responded that we didn't have to worry and that we should *trust* her. As it turned out, she was right—her grades were fine. But the secrecy nearly drove us crazy.

2. *They want to make their own decisions* concerning clothes, classes, and use of leisure time. We shouldn't be surprised at disagreements about fashions, types of friends, and curfew. And we should make reasonable compromises.

Marcee Bennett explains that their son Theo's symbol for independence was his long hair: *He didn't grow his hair long to rebel against us, but to be different. He seemed to like the reaction he got at school. I think he wanted us to like it, but we didn't. I decided to talk with him because it was becoming an issue. I told Theo that his hair wasn't worth fighting over. He would have to accept the fact that we didn't like it, and we would have to accept the fact that he did.*

3. *They may be very defensive* about youth culture—music, videos, fashions, and friends. And they will resent any im-

plication that they might be giving in to peer pressure. Clearly teens do respond to pressure from their peers—they still push their point with the argument "Everybody's doing it!" But they are adamant in their denial, honestly believing that they alone make each decision.

4. *They won't be as eager to have us around.* Although our children were changing rapidly during the junior high years, growing physically, and looking more and more like teenagers, they still welcomed our involvement in their world, as coaches, youth group sponsors, or chaperones. During the high school years, however, they may resent our involvement, except at a safe distance. It's their world, their turf, not ours.

It may be painful and we may not like to face this truth, but at this age our kids are pushing toward being on their own.

TRUST

Along with the push toward independence comes the issue of trust. If we don't trust our kids, we will find it difficult to allow them to have much freedom. Conversely, the more we trust them, the more we will be able to relax when they are out of our sight. Ironically, *trust* is a word we often hear from our teenage sons and daughters—"Don't you trust me?"

Some parents are almost paranoid about their teenagers, always assuming the worst and implying that their kids have ulterior motives, are deceptive, and are always getting into trouble. They may think this way because they believe all the negative news they read and hear about youth today. Or they may vividly remember their own teenage years. These parents often fill family discussions with pointed questions and accusations, leading to heated debates. This parenting style can cause open rebellion, with the teenagers thinking, *They think I'm guilty, so I may as well do it.*

At the other end of the parenting spectrum are mothers and fathers who seem to be wearing blinders. Certain that their darling sons and daughters wouldn't possibly do anything wrong, they allow too much freedom, ignore obvious signs of trouble, and deny reality when confronted with the truth. Some of these parents have a naive understanding of youth culture and human nature. I worked closely with high school students for many years, and I saw many of them fool their parents. Kids who have grown up in the church seem especially proficient at this. They have learned how to say the right words to parents and youth leaders and then sneak around and do as they please. When these kids get pregnant, drunk, or in trouble, their parents are shocked.

HOW TO RESPOND

A much more effective approach falls in the middle of those two extremes. As responsible and loving parents, we should have a realistic view of the world and youth culture. The world is not interested in helping us teach Christian values to our children. In fact, the opposite is true. If you want proof, watch commercials aimed at high schoolers, MTV, and a teen-oriented TV show. With each year, the pressure mounts for kids to be sexually active. Some high schools imply approval by emphasizing birth control in health classes and distributing condoms in school-based clinics. And in many schools, being a virgin is a joke. Besides having sex, high schoolers are pressured to drink and do drugs. For many kids these problems and pressures begin in junior high or sooner.

I have male friends whose daughters are approaching puberty at speeds upwards of 700 miles per hour, and when you say the word "dating," my friends get a look in their eyes that makes Charles Manson look like Captain Kangaroo.

Dave Barry

Although the pressures are great, we shouldn't assume that our kids are involved and accuse them falsely. But we shouldn't foolishly allow them to go anyplace at any time and do whatever they want. I am still surprised at what some Christian parents allow their kids to do. For example, they may set no curfew, let their child rent a motel room with another couple on prom night, let them attend a concert of a rock group known for their sexually explicit lyrics, have no accountability for how their children spend money, allow a daughter to be unsupervised at her boyfriend's house, and so forth. Nowhere is appropriate parental supervision more important than with use of the car. As mentioned earlier, in an automobile a teenager can be far from home and any adult supervision quickly and easily. We don't do our kids any favors by giving them complete, unrestricted freedom on the road.

1. Communicate

The best way to handle the issue of trust and independence is to explain to your child that you assume the best of them but that trust is easy to lose and difficult to regain. Use an example, such as an employer who will have trouble trusting a worker who has stolen from him no matter how much that employee promises never to steal again. It may take years before trust has been regained.

You also should present your rules and the reasons behind them. Then you should explain that your restrictions will loosen as your teenager displays increasing maturity and trustworthiness in each area. With an older teen, you can work out the rules together and the possible consequences for breaking them. As you present guidelines and rules, explain why these behavior barriers are important, how they have changed over the years, and that your goal is for your teenager to be self-disciplined. In a few years your teens will be away from home and on their own. Your prayer is that they will be able to make morally responsible and Christ-honoring decisions and not be swayed by emotions, sex drives, or peer pressure. You want your children to have the discipline and strength to do what is right.

One of the signs of maturity is the ability to reason and to think through the consequences of actions. When you talk things through with high school kids, you treat them like adults. Respect builds understanding and appreciation for each other. They may resist a specific rule or not agree with your reasoning, but at least they will know that you love them enough to communicate.

―――――――――――――――――――――

It's important for parents to address their kids individually and as a team. A team is more than twice as protective as an individual. It is a bulwark, a solid front. And yet only an individual can lend an intimate and sympathetic ear. We advocate protection, not overprotection. You do not always feel confident about a situation; think how much more so your teens may feel at sea in a threatening or unusual situation. They need to have back-up; a recourse to fall back upon when everything goes down crooked.

Frank Minirth, et al., Passages of Marriage (Nashville: Nelson, 1991), p. 180.

―――――――――――――――――――――

When Don Ray's daughter Donna began high school, he gave her an escape hatch for difficult situations by telling her he was always available to pick her up if she thought she was headed for trouble, no questions asked. "It gave her a sense of security, knowing that we were there. I think she called me twice."

Don adds that he tried to remind his teens that one mistake can ruin a life: *Lorna and I weren't strict, but we were narrow. We had limits, but within those limits, the kids had a lot of freedom. I also think it was good that they had us to blame when they had to explain to their friends why they couldn't go to a party, stay out past a certain hour, or do something. It took the pressure off them.*

There will be times, of course, when the issue will come down to the question of authority. In other words, your teenagers either won't understand your reasons or won't agree and will argue vociferously for their point of view and course of action. So you may have to *pull rank* and say, "I'm sorry you feel that way, but this is the way it's going to be. As your parent, it's my responsibility to do what I believe is right, before God, in this situation. So that's it—end of discussion. If you disobey, you know the consequences. I suggest that you decide to change your attitude and make the best of the situation. And remember, although you may not feel this right now, I love you."

2. Enforce

As was the case during the junior high years, you should be very careful to enforce the rules that you set. It will be painful at times to punish teenagers for a serious infraction by prohibiting them from attending a highly anticipated event, by grounding them for the weekend, or by executing another disciplinary action. It is important, however, to let your child know that you still take parenting seriously, that you have good reasons for the rules and expect them to be followed, and that you *will* follow through with enforcement.

When enforcing the rules, make the punishment fit the crime. Don't simply give a talk or tongue-lashing for a serious infraction or pronounce an extreme penalty that you will be unable to carry out.

3. Compromise

Compromise also plays an important role in allowing your high schooler to mature and move toward independence. To encourage your teens to think things through and to share their ideas and feelings, you should listen carefully and take them seriously. You should be willing to compromise whenever possible. This will demonstrate that you respect your child as a person and that you respect their ability to think and reason. It also builds trust.

There are few responsibilities in life as physically and emotionally draining as the responsibility to provide discipline. There are even fewer responsibilities that will give your kids a more solid foundation for growth and development. It is worth the effort. Life without discipline would be like a game without rules—confusing, shapeless, and you'd never even know if you were winning. Discipline is hard evidence of your love. It will save untold heartache in the future, and it will give you a yardstick by which you and your children can measure progress.

Ken Davis, How to Live with Your Kids, When You've Already Lost Your Mind (Grand Rapids: Zondervan, 1992), p. 87.

Sixteen-year-old Monica's curfew is eleven o'clock on weekends, but she wants to stay out later this Saturday because Brad is having a party after the football game, which won't be over until about ten. So Monica presents her case. Monica's mother responds by saying that she has appreciated Monica's attitude lately and the fact that Monica has consistently honored the curfew. Then she adds, "I trust you, Monica, so I'll extend the curfew till midnight. But be sure to call me when you get to Brad's house."

Fifteen-year-old Tony is aching to have the CD player he saw at Stereo Town in the mall last weekend. His mom and dad have given him permission to buy a stereo for his room if he pays for it himself, but right now he is one hundred dollars short. When Tony tells Dad about his dilemma, he explains that he'd like to buy the stereo now because it's on sale, and he mentions that he has worked hard to save the rest of the money. Dad answers, "Tony, I appreciate your attitude and the fact that you've shopped around and have been saving your money. In fact, you've shown a lot of maturity in how you've been spending your money lately— you haven't been blowing it like some kids do. So I'll lend you the hundred so that you can get the CD player." A month later, Dad surprises Tony by saying, "That CD player turned out to be a good buy for you, and you've been taking care of it and haven't been blasting us out of the house. So you can forget paying me back the hundred. I'm proud of the way you're growing up."

You shouldn't compromise on basic values and morality. Those are nonnegotiable. But be open to compromise in

160

other areas, especially if your teenager has demonstrated growing maturity and trustworthiness.

Every one of our kids began to act more grown-up once they got their driver's license. They were more cooperative and more considerate.

Bruce and Mitzie Barton

---

4. Affirm

Another vital step to take in helping your high schooler achieve independence is to affirm mature and responsible actions. Often the word *discipline* carries a negative connotation and is associated with punishment. In reality, discipline means training that perfects or molds—that's positive.

One of the most effective ways to train children of any age is to offer them rewards for positive behavior—to let them see that making responsible choices is worthwhile. When they are young, you can do this through hugs, simple gifts, treats, and privileges. During high school, however, your affirmations should grow up with the child. In other words, think about what your teenager would appreciate and what would communicate your appreciation for those responsible actions. Teenagers always enjoy having more privileges. If your teens have demonstrated responsible use of the car and respect for your rules, you could allow them to drive more often. If they have faithfully communicated the evening plans, always calling when they are going to be late, you can reward this behavior by extending the curfew. If there's a track record of using money responsibly, you could give your teenagers the budgeted amount for clothes and let them make the selections and purchases. And you can still give hugs, notes of appreciation, and verbal expressions of your love.

Parents of middle adolescents need to find a balance between supporting teenagers and allowing them to confront their own problems. If your middle adolescent daughter has a conflict with her teacher, don't jump in immediately and try to solve it for her. Help her think through what she can do. Ask leading questions. Suggest that she talk directly to her teacher to try to clear up the misunderstanding. Encourage her to talk to her school counselor or principal or other appropriate person. . . . Even when the situation seems to call for your intervention, ask your adolescent's permission first. . . . Middle adolescents need your sensitivity and encouragement but they also need to learn to work out their own problems.

Bruce Narramore and Vern C. Lewis, Parenting Teens (Wheaton, Ill.: Tyndale House, 1990), p. 159.

Remember that all of these actions help your teenagers move toward independence *and* help you deal with their growing independence.

5. Look for Help

I don't want to imply that all of this will be easy and that, by trying a few techniques, your child will automatically develop into a wonderful, Christian adult. The teenage years can be stormy, and the trip toward independence can be turbulent. In fact, you will need all the help you can get. Read up on the topic, talk with others, attend seminars, and seek counsel whenever possible. Two very important sources of help are youth ministries and other parents.

I spent thirty years working with other people's children. These kids came from a wide variety of backgrounds—many of them from good, solid, Christian homes. Yet they needed and received my friendship, counsel, teaching, and guidance. I spent several hours each week on a specific high school campus, hanging around, building relationships, and generally being available. Was that ministry effective? Today, decades removed from those youth ministry events, I continue to receive feedback on how Campus Life and my involvement helped change lives. Many of my former club kids now have teenagers of their own, and over the years they have continued to walk with Christ.

Because of the countless numbers of changed lives that I have seen, I am convinced of the vital necessity of person-centered, responsible, Christ-honoring youth ministry. Yet when Kara entered high school, little was available to her. In her high school of 2,400, she was the only student from our local church, and there were no Campus Life, Young Life, or Student Venture programs. Although she was a good kid and a strong Christian, Gail and I ached for other Christian adults to befriend Kara, men and women who would venture onto that campus as missionaries for Christ and friends of kids.

When Kara was in seventh grade, Gail and I got involved in starting the junior high ministry at church, and I started a Campus Life/JV club at her middle school. When she entered high school, the youth group was small, but we had an outstanding youth minister and ministry team. During her high school years, the group grew and became a very important part of Kara's life. I am thankful for our church and that group.

One of the best resources for parents is a solid youth ministry. Do everything you can to support the leaders. Because your high schooler wants to be more independent from you, they might not welcome your involvement as a youth sponsor. But your teenager will probably be open to building friendships with other adults. These adults can give your teen needed guidance and provide positive role models.

When Erik and Crista Veerman were in high school, they were attracted to a youth group of a church other than their own. Darian explains: *They liked the group because the leader related to them well and because most of the kids in the group were from their school. Although Paul and I encouraged them to stay involved at our church, we also encouraged them to get involved in this other youth group. Because of that group, Crista and Erik helped start a Bible study at their high school.*

Paul adds: *Summer camp was also very important. Although it was expensive to send them halfway across the country, it was worth every penny. After their "camper" years, they served on the work crew. There they saw the Christian life modeled by the counselors and other camp leaders.*

You can become an advocate for youth ministry in your church, and you can begin or help support parachurch ministries on your high school campus.

Another invaluable resource that can help during the turbulent teen years is other parents of teenagers. Talk with them, enlist their prayers, and seek their counsel. You could even start a *support group* in your church. (Don't call it that, however. Parents Together or something similar would be much better.)

Art Wittmann says: *I don't see how anyone can survive having teenagers without a strong faith in God. It also helps to talk with other Christian parents and to have neighborhood support—parents who have the same values and standards.*

Gail and I have enjoyed getting together with other parents. We've talked, prayed, and cried together about our kids. We've also learned from each other through sharing our successes, mistakes, struggles, and failures. It may be a quick lunch, dinner, or having a few couples over to the house for coffee and dessert. However you work out the details, look for ways to help and be helped by others who are struggling as you are or who have gone through these struggles a few years before. Parents can help each other.

When your teenager pushes for independence, the natural tendency is to push back. You want to hold on to your child, to keep them young, innocent, and dependent on you. You remember those eyes wide with wonder, the giggles, and the little hand in yours. But deep down, you know that your child has to grow up, just as you did—it's inevitable. You can help your teenager grow up by *communicating, enforcing, compromising, affirming, and finding help.*

LET'S THINK ABOUT IT

Warnings
- *Don't panic.* Pushing toward independence is a natural part of growing up.
- *Don't overreact* by yelling or meting out extreme and unenforceable punishments.
- *Don't give up.* Your teenager still needs your loving discipline and supervision.
- *Don't despair.* Other parents have gone through this passage and have survived—they can offer counsel.

Opportunities
- *Help your teen move toward independence* by communicating, enforcing, compromising, and affirming.
- *Work on building your relationship with your child,* moving closer to being friends and relating as adults.
- *Prepare your child for the adult world* by teaching them how to manage money, drive defensively, fulfill responsibilities, and act responsibly.
- *Put your high schooler in touch with positive Christian role models* and youth ministries that can help them grow in the faith.

Lessons

- *Middle adolescence can test both the child and parents.* Growing up isn't easy—everyone has to adjust.
- *High schoolers can be fun to be with and talk to*—they're thinking more and more like adults.
- *Parents of teenagers still have responsibility for their children.* We can't turn them over to the school, the youth minister, or anyone else. They're ours.
- *Having a teenage driver in the house can be scary and can stretch a parent's faith.* We should teach responsibility with the automobile. But we also need to keep trusting God and depending on his care.
- *Trust can be easily lost and is not easily regained.*

Resources

- *Campus Life.* This outstanding Christian magazine is for high school students. Each issue has stories and articles centering on the problems and needs of young people. Regular columns focus on personal Bible study, contemporary music, humor, and sharing faith in Christ. A special college edition is published twice a year. To subscribe, write to 465 Gundersen Drive, Carol Stream, IL 60188, or call 800-678-6083.
- Jack Crabtree, *Play It Safe* (Wheaton, Ill.: Victor, 1993). Although written specifically for youth directors, this book should also be required reading for parents of teenagers. Jack covers the spectrum of youth activities and gives practical advice on how to keep your kids and

ministry alive. Dozens of true stories keep the book interesting and motivating.

- Len Kageler, *Teen Shaping* (Old Tappan, N.J.: Revell, 1990). The focus of this book is discipline. Len describes teenagers at the early, middle, and late adolescent stages, helps parents discover their parenting style, and gives practical approaches for discipline at each stage.

- Jay Kesler and Ron Beers, eds., *Parents and Teenagers* (Wheaton, Ill.: Victor, 1984). The major sections of this nearly seven-hundred-page book are "What You Should Know about Parents," "What You Should Know about Teenagers," "Unifying Your Family," "Helping Teens Develop," "Balancing Freedom and Control," "Healing Broken Relationships," and "Handling Everyday Conflicts." The book contains hundreds of easy-to-read and practical articles written by scores of youth experts on every imaginable topic.

- Roger McIntire, *Losing Control of Your Teenager* (Amherst, Mass.: Human Resource Development Press, 1985). Dr. McIntire, a teacher, therapist, and consultant to school systems and institutions, presents "ten rules for raising an adult while keeping a friend." Geared to parents, this book is easy to read and very practical.

- Miriam Neff, *Helping Teens in Crisis* (Wheaton, Ill.: Tyndale House, 1993). As the title indicates, this book gives help for parents and youth workers for dealing with teenagers who are in crisis. Written by a counselor in a public high school, it is filled with realistic and practical advice.

- Dave Veerman, *Getting Your Kid to Talk* (Wheaton, Ill.: Tyndale House, 1994). This inexpensive paperback has 101 easy-to-use ideas for getting your child (and teenager) to talk with you.

Adjusting
Our Dreams

—————◦—————

7

Jeremy casts an imposing shadow on the athletic field. At six feet, six inches and 240 pounds, he can scan the secondary and choose the open receiver to hit with a short bullet pass or a soft, arching deep toss. When his pass protection breaks down, Jeremy can scramble out of trouble. Unusually quick and agile for his size, he outruns most of the backs during practice and has emerged as the second-leading rusher on the team. Already, colleges have been scouting this talented sophomore.

After football season ends, Jeremy plays power forward on the varsity basketball team and has been touted by local newspapers as a possible All-State selection. In the spring Jeremy plays first base, although it is rumored that he may not be playing baseball this spring. Instead, he probably will garner the romantic lead in the school musical. Jeremy's first love is music: He sings first tenor in the *a cappella* choir and plays a mean sax in the jazz ensemble.

In addition to his activities at West High, Jeremy volunteers at a local nursing home, helps lead his church youth group, and actively participates in Campus Life. Jeremy is known for his strong Christian commitment.

With all of these activities and responsibilities, you might expect Jeremy's grades to suffer. But he carries a full schedule of honors courses and all A's on his report cards. In addition, he serves as sophomore class president and will be the school's representative to Boys' State.

If you think Jeremy is too good to be true, you're right—I made him up. But he matches what many parents imagine and dream for their sons. A daughter's scenario would be similar: outstanding in athletics, academics, and student government; homecoming queen; spiritual giant; popular, beautiful, and talented in art, dance, music, and drama. Other parents may dream beyond high school: Olympian, doctor, star of the stage or screen, president of the United States.

As we rock our newborns to sleep, we wonder what they will be . . . and we dream.

We know, of course, that not all of those dreams are possible, and we're willing to settle for less. But deep in our hearts we know that *this child* will be something special!

The vast majority of our children are not dazzlingly brilliant, extremely witty, highly coordinated, tremendously talented, or universally popular! They are just plain kids with oversized needs to be loved and accepted as they are.

Dr. James Dobson, Hide or Seek (Old Tappan, N.J.: Revell, 1979), p. 47.

In reality, each child *is* special—a unique creation of our loving God and packed with their own blend of talents, gifts, abilities, and potential. The problem, however, is that the child may not match the picture in the minds of their parents, which can lead to conflicts and feelings of disappointment. One day the parents will have to adjust their dreams to match reality.

Our dreams come easily when we hold our babies in our arms. But as our children begin to grow, interact with other children, and go to school, the ideals meet reality. Parents' dream adjustments come in stages throughout the parenting process, but often they peak during the high school or college years. And the experience of coming to grips with what their kids are becoming can be painful and may catch them by surprise.

This, then, is the seventh passage of parenting: having to adjust our dreams to match the truth about our children.

THE DREAMS

To begin, let's take a closer look at the dreams. Where do they originate? What causes them? I have identified five sources.

1. Desiring the Best

All good parents want the very best for their children; thus, most of their dreams flow from that motive. They want their kids to reach their potential, to have positive self-images, to be happy and productive members of society, to build good marriages, and to have close and growing relationships with God.

Parents also remember their own mistakes in high school: lost opportunities, shortsighted decisions, and untapped potential. So they try to keep their children from repeating those mistakes and from taking detours and side roads off the highway of success.

Desiring the best for a child is certainly a positive motive.

2. Wanting Them to Be Better

The dream of my parents' generation, men and women who lived through the Great Depression, was that their children would have a better life, especially economically and educationally. Gail's parents didn't have the opportunity for higher education, so their top goal for Gail and her brother was that they would graduate from college.

It's natural for parents to want their children to be better than they were and to have a better life. These days, however, this goal has become more difficult to accomplish. Since the Great Depression, our nation's economy, with a few recessional blips here and there, has moved steadily upward. Thus it has become a struggle in many families for children to move beyond their parents on the economic scale. In fact, they may move backwards, with jobs becoming scarce in many areas.

Many parents also carry unfulfilled dreams and unmet goals from their own pasts: a sports career cut short by injury, a lost academic opportunity as a result of taking easy courses in school, a struggle to make ends meet because of marrying young, and so forth. They want better for their kids.

Children need to separate from their families and find a niche of their own ("individuate" is the technical term), but they also need to be able to come home, particularly during their late teens and early years of adulthood. We mean emotionally here rather than residentially. A young adult sometimes covets the advice and wisdom of a parent figure, particularly when facing momentous decisions or tragedy. If Mom and Dad are confused or weak about their own values, perhaps even their own individuality, once the teen takes wing, there is little to come back to.

Frank Minirth, et al., Passages of Marriage (Nashville: Nelson, 1991), p. 174.

---

3. Comparing to Society

Watch TV very long and you'll get a good idea of how the world measures success: by the wealth, good looks, fame, and power one possesses. Check out the spokespersons in the advertisements. Usually they are flawless physical specimens or celebrities. Most of the featured celebrities achieved their fame through professional sports, music, or films. Despite the fact that fame is fleeting, our culture almost worships people like Michael Jordan, Sting, and Madonna.

Consider also the rise of gambling in our country. First we had horse racing and Las Vegas. Next came dog racing, Atlantic City, offtrack betting, and a lottery or two. Now just about every state has a lottery, and on every river, a floating casino. The popularity of gambling arises from human greed and the lust for money. People ache to win millions—and will spend thousands trying. The clear message is that money can solve any problem, cure any malaise, and fulfill any dream.

It's easy to buy into these values, for ourselves and our children. Thus many parents push their kids toward lucrative careers and evaluate every choice by its earning or power potential.

4. Competing with Others

Competition is as American as apple pie. Every teen claims to be *number one;* everyone wants to be *the best.* In fact, those who come in second are considered losers. When the Buffalo Bills lost their third straight Super Bowl, the owner fired the general manager. When they lost their fourth, he made wholesale changes. Only two teams in the NFL make it to the big game each year—to make it four years in a row is amazing. Yet many see the Bills as losers.

We compete in every area. Networks broadcast a steady stream of awards shows and beauty contests. Even my subdivision honors a lawn of the month during the summer and the best-decorated homes during the Christmas season.

We also compete through our children, sincerely believing that they need to be the brightest and best. We may compete with neighbors, friends' children, or cousins and thus pressure our kids to perform. When another child wins an award or is honored instead of ours, we think, *Why did he get it?* rather than sincerely congratulating the child and his parents.

5. Building Up Self

Many parents find personal fulfillment through the successes of their kids. We feel good about ourselves when our children perform well, especially when they win a competition or succeed in an area valued by society. "That's my boy!"

says the proud Little League father as he nudges the man next to him in the stands. And Mom beams as she hears that her beautiful daughter "looks just like her mother."

It's not easy watching a son on the JV basketball team sit on the bench, seeing the honor roll in the paper with a notable exception, or talking with other parents and explaining that your daughter won't be going to college. We take our childrens' shortcomings and failures personally—our self-esteem suffers.

Most parental dreams arise from one or a combination of these five sources. Often we are unaware of their origin. At other times we may rationalize by saying that we only *desire the best* for the child, when our real motives are much more self-centered.

THE CONFLICTS

One reason the problems and pressures associated with parents' dreams for their children usually peak during high school or college is that the young person has had time to grow, mature, learn, and establish a pattern and record of accomplishments. By that time we have a pretty good idea of the direction our teenagers are heading.

If your son is five feet, seven inches, weighs 140 pounds, and sits on the bench of the freshman B football team, the chances are good that he won't be the football star you dreamed he would be. If your sophomore daughter has been struggling with her grades, she probably won't be the class valedictorian at graduation. If your son is just barely passing math, he probably shouldn't go into engineering.

My dreams for Crista and Erik had to be adjusted quite a bit in high school. Crista was really into sports when she was sidelined by a knee operation. She channeled her energy into other areas, including student government, and was class president all four years of high school. Actually the knee operation influenced her careerwise, too—she's the head student trainer in college and wants to go into physical therapy.

Erik had a very successful sophomore year playing football. Because I like football, I loved watching him play. But he didn't like it and decided to swim his junior year instead. He qualified for state, and I was psyched. The next year, however, he dropped swimming and went into music. I was a little frustrated but tried to support him in his decision. He ended up getting the lead in *West Side Story* and has become quite involved with music in college.

Paul Veerman

Another important reason for the conflicts arising at this time is that the main emotional focus of high schoolers is on identity, understanding who they are and where they fit in. During junior high they were working on *competence,* so they tried every activity and joined every club. Now in high school, they're looking for their niche, and it may not be where you want them.

Ramon really enjoys art and wants to take more art

179

classes. His father would rather that he take another science course so he can get into a good college.

Heidi has played basketball since seventh grade—it's been her favorite sport, and she has enjoyed some success on the court. But she doesn't want to go out for the team this season.

Frank has always wanted to be a surgeon. Lately, however, he has been talking about going into the ministry.

Natalie always planned on going to college and joining her parents in the family retail business. Last week she announced that she would rather go to trade school and go into electronics.

Many Christian parents have spiritual expectations as well. They may assume that their bright and enthusiastic children will become spiritual giants in high school, boldly standing for Christ and witnessing to their friends. But on a scale of 1 to 10, most Christian high school students would rate their interest as follows:

◆ Popular music	10
◆ Friends	10
◆ Prayer	1
◆ Church	1

That's not exactly what Mom and Dad envisioned.

Inside Struggles

As our dreams for our children begin to fade or change, we may go through a grieving process.

First, we deny reality and push kids even harder. Jason just wasn't cut out to be a basketball player, yet his father sent him to every camp and spoke with the coaches. Eventually the father moved his family to another town so that Jason could go to a school where he would have the chance to play more. It's tough to accept the death of a dream, so we blame coaches and teachers, ignore the obvious, and make excuses . . . and continue to push our kids to perform.

Next, we may try to bargain—with God, ourselves, or the child—hoping to delay the inevitable or reverse the course. We promise God that we will be better parents or better Christians if he will intervene on our child's behalf. We strike a bargain with ourselves—to work with the boy on his jump shot, to pay for tutoring in a specific course of study, or to try harder at family relationships. With the child, we offer *bribes:* "If you go out for football, I'll buy you a car next year" or "If you get a part in the musical, we'll go on that vacation trip we talked about." Whatever the case, bargaining is an extension of denial and a last-ditch attempt to stop what is happening or delay the inevitable.

When bargaining doesn't work, we recognize the truth and become angry. Often, our anger is directed at the child: "You didn't apply yourself! What's wrong with you, anyway?" We may become angry with God and feel singled out or cheated, especially if we compare our kids to others who have achieved much more in a certain area. We can become angry with coaches, teachers, the administration, the school system, and even the country. But we can also become angry with ourselves and second-guess past decisions: "If we hadn't moved to this city, . . ." "I knew we should have sent her to that camp. . . ." "I can't believe I let him talk me into letting him drop college algebra. . . ."

Eventually, however, we come to sorrow as we realize that for whatever reason, a dream has died. These sad feelings can be difficult to sort through because often they don't *make sense.* After all, our teenagers are still in good health, not in jail, and doing reasonably well in most areas. But it still hurts to realize that they won't fulfill our ideal for them. I know parents who have shed bitter tears over issues or choices that to outsiders seem very insignificant.

At last, we come—we hope—to the final stage, acceptance, when we will be able to accept the truth about our kids, accept them for who they are, and still have a good relationship with them.

Marcee Bennett says: *As my children got older, I had to die to some of my visions. In my mind, I expected my kids to go a certain way, marry a certain type of person, and so forth. But I couldn't hold them to my dreams. Actually, their dreams were better. They need to make their own way. It wouldn't be fair to the children to force them into my visions for them.*

Outside Struggles

Although parents may debate and argue with teachers and coaches, most of the external conflicts about dreams occur between parents and their teenagers. It may be a fight about friends, tension over next year's courses, an argument about practicing the piano, or a shouting match over grades.

Whatever the trigger, often the real conflict concerns a major difference between the parent's and child's goals.

I'm not suggesting that the young person is always right and that the parents should always give in and adjust their way of thinking. Far from it. Actually, adolescents are short-sighted—they haven't had enough life experience to enable them to understand the far-reaching consequences of their actions. They certainly aren't objective about their abilities and needs. Although they are maturing rapidly, they are still kids, governed, to a great extent, by doing whatever feels good and wanting to do it *now*. Parents have the God-given responsibility to guide their children, even middle adolescents, toward making good decisions and toward good stewardship of their gifts and talents. But we shouldn't make *unrealistic* demands. And we shouldn't be surprised by the conflicts.

HOW TO RESPOND

As much as we would like it, there's no formula for guaranteed success in this area, for dealing with our feelings, or for resolving conflicts with our kids. But here are a few steps you can take to ease the transition through this passage.

1. Check Your Values and Motives

The process begins with an honest evaluation of why you have specific dreams and goals for your child. Do you really have the child's best interest at heart? Or are you measuring success according to the world's standard? Remember John's admonition:

Stop loving this evil world and all that it offers you, for when you love these things you show that you do not really love God; for all these worldly things, these evil desires— the craze for sex, the ambition to buy everything that appeals to you, and the pride that comes from wealth and importance—these are not from God. They are from this evil world itself. And this world is fading away, and these evil, forbidden things will go with it, but whoever keeps doing the will of God will live forever. (1 John 2:15-17, TLB)

Some parents are so impressed with their kids that they don't give guidance. Others are so depressed that they don't give encouragement. Don't write your kids off or give up. Keep guiding, encouraging, and loving them.

Bruce Barton

Jack Crabtree shares his experience with parental dreams: *I was stunned the night my son told me that he wanted to quit the high school football team. When I grew up, participation in team sports was a premier social value. Since I never won a varsity letter, I felt as though my unfulfilled dream was coming true when I saw my son starting on the varsity football team as a fifteen-year-old sophomore.*

But it wasn't his dream. In fact, all my reasoning with him

184

about the benefits of sticking with the team did not change his decision. He finally convinced me when he said that while he knew most other kids wanted to be where he was, the whole football scene wasn't important to him. He wanted to get a job and pursue individual sports instead.

The sorrow I felt that fall was the death of my dream and the realization that my son and I shared different values regarding team sports like football. During that season and the next two (without football), I learned that a young man's self-esteem can develop quite well without fighting over an odd-shaped ball.

Today my son continues to ski and surf for fun and exercise on two undamaged knees. He has no regrets about quitting football—and now that time has taught me a valuable lesson about not forcing my values on my kids, neither do I.

Another good question to ask is Whose needs am I meeting? Be honest. Maybe you're pushing in a certain area because you failed there or fell short of your dream for yourself. One dad told me that he was unhappy with his freshman daughter's grades for the first semester—he knew she could do better. She had a B in honors English, a B in world history, a B in biology, an A– in geometry, and so forth. He was disappointed with the grades until he put them in perspective. "Once I saw that she wouldn't be the valedictorian," he said, "I thought, *Hey, those are pretty good grades in some pretty difficult subjects. She's doing great!*" Once he saw the larger picture, his daughter came into focus.

Perhaps you're pushing for specific success because you always wanted to be part of the *in crowd* in high school.

185

Maybe you just want to feel better about yourself and your parenting ability.

First, take an honest look at yourself.

2. Affirm Their Talents and Gifts

Look carefully at your teenagers to determine their talents, gifts, and motivated abilities. They may have an undiscovered talent in one area or undeveloped potential in another. Most high schools offer a broad range of curricular and extracurricular activities. If your teenagers aren't doing well in one endeavor, encourage them to try another.

I spent a lot of time in high school trying to be an athlete because football and basketball players were highly valued. Yet today I spend most of my time writing. I'm sure that I would have enjoyed working on the high school paper and taking a creative-writing or journalism class.

Darrell Harris, the president and cofounder of Star Song Communications, writes:

> We were asked at school to prepare our elective choices for the next four years, taking the first real steps of defining career direction. I had brought home the folder with all the information and options.
>
> Perhaps we only spent an evening or two at the endeavor. But I remember filling out those forms as if it took up the better part of a couple of weeks. Daddy seemed to really enjoy it, and so did I because, in our kitchen during those evenings, the gateways to a million possibilities seemed to open up to me.

"If you could be anything you want, what would it be?"
he asked. His question seemed to imply that I could become
president of the United States or king of the world if I so
chose. But having begun to play the clarinet in the school
band, and being fascinated with the junior high band
leader with his baton and knowledge of the world of
composers and instruments, I answered, "A band director."

Daddy never batted an eye. If my answer brought him
any displeasure, I never knew it. Without hesitation, he
put "band" in one of the elective blanks for each year—all
the way through high school. (Gloria Gaither, ed., What
My Parents Did Right, Nashville: Star Song, 1992, p.
102.)

Your child may enjoy hunting and fishing, being an
athletic trainer, working on cars, making crafts, collecting
sports memorabilia, taking pictures, writing, making sets for
dramatic productions, tutoring children, teaching Sunday
school, working on the yearbook, learning karate, serving as
campus reporter for a local newspaper—there's no limit to
the number of possibilities for finding success, enjoyment,
and affirmation.

Greg Johnson and Mike Yorkey write:

The lesson, of course, is to channel your children's early
bents or natural talents in much the same way as a river
flows: As long as it's flowing in the right direction, there's
no need to dam up the river or divert it to another
direction. Go with the flow, but challenge your offspring

to branch out as well. Remember, you don't have a lock on knowing which direction God wants that water to travel. You just have the responsibility to guide your children safely through the river channel. (Faithful Parents, Faithful Kids, Wheaton, Ill.: Tyndale House, 1993, p. 66)

Look for areas of interest, hidden talent, and untapped potential in your teenager.

3. Hold Them Loosely

In chapter 6, we looked at the issue of independence. In addition to identity, independence is the other major issue for high schoolers. It's tough letting our children go, but we have to help them grow up and stand on their own. We can't let something go if we're holding on with clenched fists. Yet that's how many parents relate to their teenagers. They know what's best for their children and that's it—period!

"He had so much potential. Now he just is too painful to have in my house anymore. In fact, I hate him and never want to see him again!" yelled Johnny's mother as he tearfully listened to her angry words.

Tommy is a difficult teenager. He takes drugs, sells his body, and seldom comes home on weekends. Tommy's mother was at the end of her rope. She wanted him out of the house.

Through tears, Tommy told me about his life. Mom had expected too much from him. "She always tells me that I have so much *potential.* I tried desperately for a while, leading all my neighborhood friends to the Lord, memorizing chapters of the Bible. I was at the top of my class academically and in all kinds of sports—being perfect everywhere I went. I never could meet her expectations of me because it never was good enough, so I finally gave up. I always thought she hated me, but now I know."

Today, Tommy is in a detox center trying to "dry out," while his mom has taken on a new crusade to rid society of all pornography. Tommy's mom tried to find her own life through her son. Her constant pressure, expectations, and correction were deadly tools that alienated her son from her.

I am beginning to realize that many times we parents take on too much responsibility for our children. Yes, we are entrusted with these precious lives, but we must remember whose children they really are. These children are God's!

Kirby Hanawalt, a marriage and family counselor for Greater Vancouver (Canada) Youth for Christ

---

Lew and Dottye Luttrell shared an experience of dream adjustment. Their son Kirk was a sophomore at Taylor University. All through high school, Kirk had planned to be an aerospace engineer, and he had taken all the courses to move him in that direction. One and a half semesters into college, he announced to Mom and Dad that he was changing to Christian education. Lew said: *This was a real struggle for us, especially me because I had been very proud that my son was going to be an engineer. Yet we remembered that we had given Kirk back to God when he was born, so we said, "Lord, if you want him in Christian ed, it's OK." Later, in a parents meeting on campus, a Bible-department professor gave a strong devotional on Hannah's experience with Samuel. She emphasized that we must hold our children with open hands, giving them the freedom to serve God. As she spoke those words, she placed her hands in front of her, palms up. It was a very graphic gesture and confirmed the fact that Kirk was really in God's hands, not ours.*

I didn't realize that my parents' dreams were tied up in me until after my dad's death a few years go. In his reflections he wrote: *We moved to Rockford the year Dave started kindergarten, and during those early years, I took him and his brothers to several high school football games—hopefully to get them vitally interested in the game. So when Dave went out for football at Roosevelt Junior High as a ninth grader, I was filled with anticipation. But so many things are taught me the hard way. Dave was cut from the squad, and my world started falling apart. Shortly afterward he tried out for (and got) a part in an operetta and did a good job. I had to learn that each child has to do his own thing and should not be pushed. The next year, however, when Dave was four inches taller and fifty pounds heavier, he won his football letter on the sophomore team and later went on to play regularly as a junior and senior.* Looking back at that time, I have to say honestly that I never felt pushed by Mom or Dad. Certainly they were guiding, but I felt a lot of freedom to choose. They held me with open hands.

Don't grasp, push, or dominate your teenager. Hold your child, and your dreams, loosely.

4. Guide Them with Love

Even if they don't realize it, your teenager needs you. You and your spouse know your child better than anyone else, and you have wisdom drawn from your years of education and experience. In addition, you want what's best for your child. If you've been honest about your feelings, you've purged the self-centered motives and can give valuable counsel for their future.

Matthew, our oldest, has always been better with actions than words.

Every year on Mother's Day, our church gives each of the moms in the worship service a red carnation. One year I decided to have the little kids who come to the front for the children's message be the delivery crew. After giving my brief devotional, I asked them to each take a carnation and find a mom they could give it to. They were to keep coming back for another until all the mothers had received a flower. I was busy handing out flowers when I noticed a rather large hand reaching out for one. I looked up into my seventeen-year-old, almost-grown son's eyes. He had walked forward from his spot in the back pew. With every eye fixed on him, he took the flower from me and walked back to where his mother was sitting, tears flowing down her cheeks. He bent over and gave her a kiss as he handed her the flower. When it's really their expression of love, you just can't beat it.

Neil Wilson

So don't be afraid to give it. But give it with love. Guiding with love means:
- Choose a positive attitude—don't harp on the negatives
- Be realistic about your child's talent and potential
- Reduce expectations—whether it's homecoming queen, lead in the play, star on the team, editor of the yearbook, president of the class, or valedictorian, there's usually only one per school, so relax
- Be honest with your child about your feelings and thoughts—let your kid understand your reasoning; try to broaden their perspective
- Stay engaged—encouraging, compromising, or backing off when necessary

When Kara was a freshman in high school, she decided not to take chorus. We knew how much she enjoyed singing, but we gave in because she had a full schedule of classes and was on the volleyball team. The next year, she wanted to do the same, but over her protests, Gail and I insisted that she join the choir—we knew Kara had talent and wanted her to develop this area of her life. So she did take chorus and she loved it. She stayed in choir the rest of her high school career.

It's not easy knowing when to direct and when to back off, especially when you're afraid that you might be trying to meet your own needs through your child. With difficult decisions, you and your spouse may want to consult with other parents who have gone through a similar process. Although your teenager is unique, the process will be the same, and these trusted friends will provide valuable counsel.

The goal of guiding with love is to move your child in the right direction while building a more adult relationship with your teen.

Babs Swanson says: *My relationship with Brooke is much different from my relationship with my mother during these years. My mother and I did not appreciate each other when I was in high school, but Brooke counts me as a close friend. Often I wonder what is healthy for her, and for me, and I try to establish the appropriate boundaries.* Babs has been able to build a positive relationship with her teenage daughter.

Guide your high school child in the right direction, with love.

5. Keep Talking

Grades are important, so you will have an argument with your teenager if their grades start to slip. Involvement in school activities is important, so you may have a conflict with your teenagers if they want to pull out and get a job or just sit around the house. Preparing for the future is important, so you may have a battle or two on your hands when you discuss courses of study and career options. But in all of these discussions and disagreements, even when you have to insist on your way, keep the communication channels open. Don't lose your cool and lose the child.

During these discussions, listen carefully to what your teenagers are saying. Even if their reasoning makes no sense and is comical, don't laugh or respond with sarcasm. Take what they say seriously and bring them up to your level of maturity—don't slide down to theirs.

If you reach an impasse, you may have to express your authority and tell them what to do, but do it calmly and with respect. Then trust God that your child will choose a good attitude and obey you.

Keep the communication lines open.

6. Keep Praying

When our dreams die, so do we, a little bit. Ask God to give you the grace to deal with the way things are rather than the way you wish they were and the ability to see the big picture, not the minuscule problem.

Keep praying for your teenager, too. Remember, high school is tough, especially considering the temptations and peer pressure. Young people feel hurt and confused when their dreams die. Pray that your child will build self-esteem on the fact that they are loved—by God and by their parents.

Dreams are great—in them we imagine idealized bodies, minds, and successes. But dreams aren't real and need to be adjusted when we face reality. As you realize the truth about your teenagers, you will need to change your focus and expectations, *check your values and motives, affirm your teenagers' talents and gifts, hold your child loosely, guide them with love, keep talking,* and *keep praying.* Turn this passage into one of joy and hope for the future.

LET'S THINK ABOUT IT

Warnings

- *Don't project your needs and desires onto your teenager.* Realize that they are unique individuals and quite different from you.
- *Don't set unrealistic expectations for your young person or yourself.* Affirm your child's talents and rejoice in their successes.
- *Don't give up and allow total freedom.* Your teenager still needs your insight, counsel, and guidance.
- *Don't win the battle and lose the child.* When you argue with your teen, fight fairly and respect their thoughts, ideas, and reasons.

Opportunities

- *Use this passage of parenting to teach you about yourself.* Consider why you are disappointed with your child, and analyze your motives for pushing your teen in certain directions.
- *Turn conflicts over performance and goals into occasions to communicate.* Work at building an adult relationship with your teenager.

- *Stretch your faith by turning each issue over to God and trusting him for the outcome* (see James 1:2-7).
- *Help your teenager personalize faith.* Guide your maturing child to seek God's will and be ready to accept it (see Philippians 2:12-13).

Lessons

- *Each child is unique and not a copy of either parent.* We must affirm what is unique about each child and help them discover their latent abilities, talents, and gifts.
- *Dreams die hard*—the truth can be painful. God's values and standards are important; the world's are not. We must resist thinking and acting as though money, sex, physical beauty, prestige, and power mean everything.
- *We must hold our children with open hands*—they belong to God, not us.

Resources

- Diane Eble and Richard Hagstrom, *Discover Your Best Possible Future* (Grand Rapids: Zondervan, 1993). Filled with real-life examples, this book lives up to its billing: *A Step-by-Step Guide to Choosing a College, a Major, a Career.* With charts and easy-to-use assessment tools, the authors help students discover their motivated abilities to help them plan for the future.
- *Life Application Bible* (Wheaton, Ill.: Tyndale House, 1988). This supercharged, user-friendly study Bible has ten thousand notes and is available in *The Living Bible,* King James Version, New Revised Standard Version,

New International Version, and New King James Version translations of the Scriptures. In addition to explaining the text and answering cultural and theological questions, the notes apply Bible texts by confronting readers with the right questions and motivating them to action. This adult Bible would be an excellent gift for juniors or seniors in high school as they move into adulthood.

- David R. Veerman, *Youth Evangelism* (Wheaton, Ill.: Victor, 1988). Written to mobilize Christian adults to reach high school students for Christ, this book will explain how to relate to middle adolescents and will provide many ideas for how you and your teenager can share the gospel with your teenager's friends.

- R. C. Sproul, *Choosing My Religion* (Orlando, Fla.: Ligonier Ministries, 1993). Dr. Sproul is an outstanding evangelical theologian *and* communicator. This two-video set contains five compelling lessons to prepare young people for the false philosophies that hit them from every direction in the world today. Focusing on truth, God, sin, salvation, and Christian ethics, these lessons help kids build a solid foundation for their faith. The videos are ideal for use at home or with a group of students.

Letting Go

8

The Top Ten Advantages of Your Child Leaving Home

10. You will significantly reduce your number of bank accounts and investments.
9. You will finally see the floor of the bedroom.
8. You will get to redeem all of your airline frequent-flyer miles.
7. You will be able to use the bathroom much sooner.

6. You will begin to worry about crime in another city.

5. You will learn how to wire money.

4. You will look at baby albums again and again.

3. You will learn to read between the lines of your student's letters.

2. During vacation breaks, you will feel very old and conservative.

1. At orientation and parents' weekend, you will meet many other people just as confused and broke as you.

Whether it's going to college, into the military, or into the workforce, leaving home is a significant passage for both parent and child. For the young person, leaving home means becoming an adult—being out in the world with the freedom to make decisions, released from childhood restraints. It's exciting, exhilarating, and a little scary. For parents, this passage is no laughing matter. Many dread this day, struggle when it comes, and grieve long afterward.

One mother, Rachel Ringenberg, said to me, "When we sent our oldest child, Brent, off to college, I was a basket case. I knew our family would never be the same again."

A few months into the new school year, the mother of one of Kara's friends shared that she hadn't stopped crying since her daughter left for college.

Ken Davis shares a father's perspective: *I remember vividly the day Traci was born. It could have been yesterday. I looked and fell instantly in love with a little package of life. She was the most beautiful thing in the world. The doctor asked me if I would like to hold her. "No," I said. If I touched her, I knew she would break. But the doctor assured me she could survive the ordeal and laid her in my arms.*

How light she was! How beautiful she appeared through the soft blur of my tears! Then I made a terrible mistake. I blinked. In an instant eighteen years went by.

When I opened my eyes, she was still in my arms; tears still in my eyes. But she was no longer a baby. She was a beautiful young woman, and I was saying good-bye. Leaving Traci in a small college dorm room was one of the hardest things I have done in my life ("The Punch Line," Ken Davis Newsletter, *9, no. 1, November 1993, p. 2).*

The following list might more accurately express the feelings of these parents and thousands of others each year:

The Top Ten Disadvantages of Your Child Leaving Home

10. *You keep expecting to hear or see your child, but they aren't there.*

9. *You have to feed the dog, shovel the walk, and cut the grass.*

8. *You have to keep buying tissue.*

7. *Your long-distance telephone bill skyrockets.*

6. *You worry about your child's classes, dates, spiritual life, etc.*

5. *You have to keep walking past that empty room.*

4. *You set one less place at the table.*

3. *Your house is much too quiet.*

2. *You struggle to fill the hole in your life and family.*

1. *You lose a lot of sleep.*

I didn't know how I would react when Kara left for college. Many years before, I had heard stories of how difficult it was for some parents to say good-bye to their kids, but I didn't think it would be that big a deal for me. Then my brother and sister-in-law Paul and Darian drove from Connecticut to drop off their twins, Erik and Crista, at Wheaton College. Paul and Darian stayed with us and talked about their feelings of loss and sadness, and I began to sense what I might go through when my time came. But nothing totally prepared me for the experience.

It began for me at graduation. Kara had enjoyed a great senior year. In fact, all four years had been good—not too tough and filled with activities and accomplishments. But suddenly on that bright and windy day in June, as she walked across the platform and received her diploma, those days were over, and I knew that soon she would be gone. Misty-eyed, I fought back the tears as I congratulated Kara and hugged her close. During the following hours and days, I thought back on her life, my hopes and dreams for her, and what we had experienced together. Then I expressed many of my thoughts and feelings in this poem that I presented at our open house in her honor:

One glorious May
in seventy-five,
God said yes, and
we came alive.

Five pounds of love

our peanut she
To Ardmore home
the family now three

Through all night cries
and feedings she grew,
Johnny Jump-up, first steps,
and words so new . . .

The poem continues to trace her life through school, then concludes:

It's gone so quickly
but we're aware
Of God's gentle guidance
and answered prayer.

Now a tall, lovely woman,
Christian leader with dreams
Moves on with her life
or so it seems.

But at this life passage
please, Kara, know
That Mom and Dad's love
will never let go!

Even now as I read those last words, tears come to my eyes as I think of our little girl, almost grown and away from home.

I wasn't surprised entirely by my emotions, but I was surprised by their depth. Jerry Jenkins captures the feelings exactly in a letter to Dallas, his oldest son: *And so it has come down to this: You're going, really going. Oh, you'll be back. It isn't as if I will never see you again. But when you return, you'll come as a guest. For all practical purposes, you are gone for good.*

Though you'll always remain in my heart and be a member of our family, nothing will be the same. While I may finance your lifestyle temporarily, you are now your own person, making your own decisions, disciplining or not disciplining yourself.

It's stunning to realize that the clichés are true. All those platitudes I heard last week, when you were born, are now indisputable. "Hang on to every moment, every day," I was told when I showed you off as our new arrival. "Before you know it, they'll be gone" (As You Leave Home, *Colorado Springs: Focus on the Family, 1993, pp. 3–4*).

JOY

When a child leaves home, parents' feelings are mixed. Certainly there is joy, and so many reasons for it.

High school graduation is a significant milestone and a cause for joyous celebration. It is made even more meaning-ful by school awards and honors and the well-wishes and gifts of relatives and friends. Actually, graduation is the end of a long process. In junior high grades were important because they would determine what a student could take in high school. In high school grades were important because they would determine what a student could do or where they could go afterward. So at high school graduation ceremonies, parents breathe a collective sigh of relief: *We've passed. The pressure's off. We did it! Hooray!*

We rejoice with our sons and daughters as they receive the heartfelt congratulations of family and friends. Many parents of eighteen year olds, however, experience the opposite kind of emotion. Their kids have dropped out, spaced out, or freaked out. They continue to struggle with shattered dreams and broken hearts. But most students are moving out and beyond high school.

There is also joy because our graduates exhibit a sense of maturity. They certainly *look* grown-up. They have survived junior high, driver's education, the prom, and peer pressure. At this point we can feel that they are turning out OK—maybe we did some things right after all.

Joy also comes at the college campus, military base, or new job. Young men and women thrill with excitement for the new experiences ahead and feel ready for the challenges.

When we took Kara to college, Gail and I enjoyed the orientation process, hearing from the president of the college, talking with the deans and teachers, touring the campus, meeting her roommate and many other parents, and getting her settled in the dorm. Those few days were packed with seminars, socials, and special events. It was a fun time for all three of us.

The Luttrells' kids, Jennifer and Kirk, seemed quite ready for college. When Lew and Dottye dropped each of them off, they waited around for the warm good-byes. In both cases the kids said, in effect, "We have friends here and stuff to do . . . so we'll see you." Mom and Dad got the message and left.

Our kids may harbor a little apprehension about being on their own in a new situation, but usually their exhilaration will overshadow any anxiety they may be feeling. Or they will mask their fears. They are, after all, independent and on their own. Even amid the apprehension, it is a time of joy.

SORROW

Most parents expect to be happy about a child graduating from high school and moving on with life. What surprises them the most is the sorrow, the almost overwhelming feeling of sadness when they drive away, leaving sons and daughters behind.

Saying Good-bye

Mitzie Barton explains that, during Kari's junior year in high school, she would sit in the stands, watching Kari play basketball, and talk with the parents of seniors on the team. These parents talked about their feelings and what they were doing to prepare themselves for the trauma of their daughters' leaving home. "Practice going by the empty bedroom," they advised. "Don't miss anything—games, programs, etc.—so you'll have no regrets." Mitzie followed their advice and thought she was prepared. She knew it would be tough. She also knew that she wanted to pray with Kari just before she left and had rehearsed her final speech. But it didn't work out the way she planned. Mitzie says: *I wanted to pray and give my little talk before leaving her on campus and flying home, but I was just too emotional. I realized then that I could do nothing else. I just had to trust God for her.* As the husband of a friend drove her to the airport, she cried the whole time. *That poor man driving me around didn't know what to do with me. And the tears would come and go. I thought it would subside. Even months later when one of Kari's favorite songs would come on the radio, I would think of her singing along with it and tears would come again.*

Only a few months into the pregnancy, Sandy began to cramp up and pass blood. I rushed her to the hospital, and within the hour, she delivered our child, Jonathan, who was much too small to live. I held him, and all the emotions that I had been so diligent in controlling seemed to flood out of me. I thought I would never feel any emotion toward this little child, but as he lay lifeless in my hands, I cried out to God for him. It tore me up inside as I handed my child back to the nurse and she carried him away.

When we lost Jonathan, I got a glimpse into the deep pain that we as parents must all experience. When a child dies, goes to the university, or moves away from home, parents experience the pain of letting go. Our only hope was to turn to God in our pain and ask him to take care of little Jonathan.

Years later, with two healthy children, I realize that parenting is each day a process of letting go. When our children enter grade school, leave for camp, go to college, or marry, we must let go. Because I know that God is taking care of little Jonathan, now I know that God can take care of Ryan and Erynn.

Teach me how to let go into your arms, dear Lord.

Kirby Hanawalt

~~~~~~

Neil and Sherrie Wilson's oldest son, Matt, enlisted in the Air Force during his junior year in high school, so they had a year to get used to the idea. Neil remembers: *It was a different kind of leaving, an unexpected form of letting go. Matt's choice was neither impulsive nor rebellious. He had demonstrated to us that his skills and interests were primarily hands-on. The idea of four more years of classroom academics had little appeal, but training and working with tools and machines sounded great. The more we learned about his choice, the more we felt it fit him.*

For us, letting go had a strange finality. It wasn't like sending a child off to school, knowing that they could come home to us almost at will. If basic training proved to be too difficult, we would not be able to send him bus fare. We weren't setting a child free; we were letting him enter a different system of restraints. Also, in the back of our minds lurked the idea that we might be releasing our child to step into harm's way. Suddenly the military details of the daily news took on a new immediacy and intimacy. The flag became a symbol of cherished values.

For our two other children, big brother's departure came with heartwarming tenderness. We all endured the lip trembling at the bus stop, but the kids wept as the Greyhound pulled away. All of us sat in the car and cried together for a while. The moment was an intense mixture of love and emptiness.

I thought about the twins leaving for a year. Actually, I cried so much before they left that, when the time came, I was more excited than sad. I was excited about their going to Wheaton College and about what they would experience there. I had also come to the point where I thought, *I've done all I can do,* and I realized that they were mature and strong Christians and ready to leave home.

Darian Veerman

It has happened to us before, of course, in small doses—sending children off to kindergarten, driving them to summer camp, putting them on the bus to the grandparents' house. But each time we knew the kids would be coming home in the afternoon, a few days, or a couple of weeks. When we drop them off at their new residence or send them off on the bus, we know that it will be weeks and maybe months before they're home again, and then just for a visit.

One woman explained that she had cried just about the whole three-hour trip home from the university, and she added, "Why do I feel like someone has just died?"

A Sense of Loss

A final cause for sorrow is our profound sense of loss. In a sense, the woman was right: Someone has died. The child of the past is gone: the cute and cuddly baby and toddler, the inquisitive and innocent kindergartner and elementary schooler, the changing and challenging junior higher, and the rapidly growing and accomplishing senior higher. The child, kid, and student are gone, and in their place stands an adult, a grown-up person. We grieve the loss.

> Walking in your child's shoes helps, too. I would encourage parents that when they send a kid away to college: Mom, spend just an overnight with your daughter, if possible, on her floor [and Dad, with your son, on his floor]. If you can walk in her shoes and see the people she's talking about and the places she's talking about, and you can envision it there, it helps. Otherwise, you feel as though you've sent her off to Timbuktu, never-never land, completely away from you. It will be better for all of you all the way around.
>
> *Karen Voke*

Marcee Bennett explains that her daughter, Lynn, became an independent adult during college, especially after going on a six-month development project to a remote village in Honduras. "I had to come to terms with the fact that Lynn doesn't need me anymore," she said. "It's nice to be needed. That's part of the loss."

Mixed with our grief is a measure of regret, looking back and considering what we might have done better in rearing our children and in preparing them for life on their own in the world. Many parents feel tremendous guilt as they reflect on the past and wonder where the time went: the father who was always out of town and missed many of his son's school activities and games; the mother whose time was consumed by the smaller children, causing her to neglect her older daughter; the couple who always seemed to be arguing about money; the Christian worker who invested time in the ministry and ignored the family. They had good intentions about changing their lifestyles, but time slipped past, and now it's too late. These parents grieve their lost opportunities.

Leaving Erik and Crista in Illinois and driving back to Connecticut was very sad for me. But I was sad for myself, not for my kids. I was happy for them, but they were gone and our lives would change. I knew I would never have that same relationship with them again.

Paul Veerman

NEW ERAS AND NEW BEGINNINGS

We are sad because we sense the passing of an era in our lives.

Now, instead of being parents of a young family or even of teenagers, we have a child *in college* or *away from home.* That's the official introduction into the older generation. No matter how much we try to deny the aging process through makeup, hairstyles, clothes, and exercise, slowly and steadily we have been getting older. Each child leaving home reminds us of that tough truth. Bob Childress says, "Until I had a kid in college, I still saw myself as a recent college graduate. Then I realized that I was getting old."

New Family Structure

We also have passed through an era in the life of the family. As Rachel Ringenberg said, the family will *never be the same again.*

The family structure and dynamics change. My family has only four: mother, father, and two children. Kara's absence leaves the family 25 percent short—that's quite a difference. And it leaves Gail and me with only one child at home. The other day at dinner, Dana noticed that both of our chairs were turned toward her—our focus was divided by Kara no longer, and we were concentrating totally on Dana and what had happened during her day at school.

A New Era for Our Children

We also know that life will never be the same again for that graduate. They are growing up and, thus, away from us. We have had to let go at each of the parenting passages, but leaving home and getting married are the biggest steps. Career, marriage, and children loom on the horizon. From this point on, our children will learn, grow, and mature more than at any other time as they tackle new and difficult subject matter, develop their own views, and confront real life.

"Where is your son applying for college?" I was sick of hearing that question at every social and church gathering. I felt awkward with my degrees from two universities, trying to explain that my son wasn't making plans for college. But quite frankly, he wasn't ready for college. He was an excellent worker when it came to physical labor, but he seemed to learn better by experience than by reading a book.

So we made the decision that rather than attend college right out of high school, he would get a job learning a construction trade. He moved to another city, several states away, and got a room with a family we knew. He would have increasing independence with some supervision from our friends. The plan was that after a year or two of learning the trade, he would make some decisions about his future education.

After six months on the job, however, he was asking about making college applications and setting his own course. Going to work in the "real world" had given him a new appreciation for the importance of an education. Struggling with paying his own bills, he had learned the value of earned dollars.

The decisions we made with our son were absolutely the best for him. Doing what best fits the young person's skills and interests shouldn't make parents feel embarrassed. In the long run, "working your way to college" may be a smarter track for a large number of young people.

Jack Crabtree

Neil Wilson tells of the changes in his son after basic training: *For Matt, the sudden transposition to a new world came as a shock. We didn't realize the depth of his experience until he came home for the first time and stood in the entryway weeping. Matt's personal character had stood up well to the usual rigors of basic training, but two remarkable transformations had come almost overnight. As if waiting to bloom under the surface, the faith that simply had been around him suddenly became intensely personal to our son. The struggle of being a pastor's kid had made his own relationship with Christ hard to sort out; now it came into startling clarity. Along with it came a new appreciation for what his home was worth. As parents, we have to offer the best we can. But the scary part is not knowing if or when our kids will ever make it on their own!*

In addition to new experiences, the recent high school graduate's personal rights will increase considerably: Eighteen year olds can vote, get married, and enlist in the army. When kids live at home, we parents usually have a pretty good idea of where they are and what they are doing. We set the rules; we're in charge. On the college campus, on the military base, or in the community, it's a different story. They are far away from our watchful eyes and restrictive rules. This increase in freedom and independence is a big change for the late adolescent—and for the parents.

Changing Relationships

Another poignant change occurs in the relationship we enjoy with a son or a daughter. We have seen the change coming, but now it's almost here. The boy or girl isn't a child or a kid anymore—they are a *young adult*. Thus, the relationship changes from strictly parent-to-child to parent-to-peer.

―――――――――――――――――

I have urged you never to be a quitter, never to give up, to stay at the task even when the outlook is bleak. Now I want to clarify that this means you are on your own. I have not abandoned you, but I have cut you loose. And just as it is important for me to let you go and make your own mistakes, so it is vital that you not see me or our home as a crutch. I am not a way station that would keep you from building your own muscle. My door is shut so you'll know I believe you can solve your own problems, find your own solutions, develop your own strategies.

I am, of course, still your friend, so if and when I can help you as a friend would, I am here. And when you need an ear, I'm here. When you need a loan—not a gift—I'm here.

Jerry B. Jenkins, As You Leave Home (Colorado Springs: Focus on the Family, 1993), pp. 15–16.

―――――――――――――――――

Children are expected to *obey* mother and father (Ephesians 6:1). This command applies to boys and girls under their parents' care. Obviously, the situation changes when children get married or live on their own and are self-sufficient. College marks a time of transition, sort of a halfway house on the way to adulthood. College-age children are still under their parents' authority, but that begins to change, gradually, as they move ever closer to total independence. Children should always *honor* their parents (Exodus 20:12; Ephesians 6:2), treating them with dignity and respect and caring for them in their old age. Children never outgrow their responsibility to honor—but soon they won't have to obey.

These changes in life and relationship can be tough for a parent to handle.

CONFUSION

In addition to feeling joy and sorrow, parents in this passage feel confused by their feelings and their changing roles.

Many parents don't know what to do with their ambivalent feelings. They cannot understand why they can't seem to shake their sorrow. They struggle with their sense of loss and guilt.

One woman told me that her son caused her so much trouble in high school that she couldn't wait for him to leave. She felt guilty that she wasn't feeling sad like many other parents and figured she must have been a poor mother. But she said that when her son came home from college, "He was different, better. I actually enjoyed having him around." Then, when he left again, she felt sad to see him go.

This *mixture* of feelings—joy, sadness, guilt, hope, fear— is confusing. Parents are happy for their kids and hopeful for their future; but they are fearful too. And they can't help but wonder if the kids were ready for this big step in their lives. Will they go to church? Will they say no to premarital sex? Are they self-disciplined enough to get up, go to class or work, and study on their own? Will they find friends? Will they be happy? Will they be safe? When will I see them again?

Karen Voke shares: *I never thought I would ever get out of the country, let alone my kids. And yet there was Julie, going to Europe on a humanities tour for six weeks. I remember taking her to the airport and thinking, "Good Lord, please watch over her because there's no way that I can even communicate with this child for the next six weeks." That huge plane was taking her away.* Seeing your kids go off on their own can be scary.

Parents also are confused by their changing roles, and they don't know how to act and react. It seemed a lot easier when the kids lived at home. Even during the turbulent junior high years and the push-for-independence senior high years, everyone knew who was in charge. But starting now, the kids no longer will live at home, at least for much of the year. Except in the military, they will operate as their own *bosses,* setting curfews, choosing entertainment and other leisure-time activities, deciding when to get involved and when to decline, and managing their time and money.

When we went to visit Kari at her summer job in California, she showed us around. It was her turf—we were the visitors. The next year when we visited her at school, we let her make all the decisions about our schedule—restaurants, activities, and so forth. It felt strange, but actually, we were just treating her like the adult she was becoming.

Bruce Barton

Parents wonder where their lines of authority begin and end, how they should guide and direct their children's lives from a distance, and how they should act when the kids return home.

Larry Kreider, who lived in Houston at the time, took his son Brett to John Brown University in Siloam Springs, Arkansas, hundreds of miles away. About four weeks later, he and Susan attended the local high school homecoming game. *A bunch of us from church decided that we were going to sit together at the game. At halftime, someone yelled out, "There's Brett!" He had been homesick and had decided to drive all night with a friend to be here for homecoming. As he walked closer, somebody else yelled out, "He's got a ring in his ear!"*

So there we are. We haven't seen our son in four weeks, we've sent him away to school, and now he's got an earring. Obviously we couldn't make a big deal out of it there. But later we asked him what it meant. It was nothing more than an expression of his identity—a very small "rebellion" compared to other possibilities.

Adjusting to the changes in our children—vast changes that occur without our involvement—is one of the challenges of this passage. With little control over their actions and choices, we have to trust our own parenting efforts, trust our sons and daughters, and trust the Lord. But still we have sleepless nights.

Jane Adams writes:

> *I tossed restlessly as the wind whistled through the trees outside my bedroom window, surprised by my sleeplessness. I thought of my son and daughter, finally settled in college dormitories on opposite ends of the continent. It had been a long, wearying journey getting them this far, so why couldn't I sleep?*
>
> *I got up and went into their rooms, banishing the silence with a flurry of shaking, dusting, and sweeping, stopping now and then to examine the discards of their childhood— outgrown clothes, old term papers, even, in a corner, a tattered teddy bear. It had always comforted me, that annual autumn rite, as if by changing the linen on their beds and lining their bureau drawers, I was making a fresh start for them. But that night the familiar tasks seemed futile. I was troubled by the idea that there was some essential parental task I had neglected, like taking them to the dentist or teaching them to say "Please" and "Thank you." But their teeth and their manners were sound, so it could not be that. And it occurred to me that I was refurbishing and repairing*

a past they had already put behind them—that although they would be returning to this house, to these rooms, they would not be living in them again, merely passing through. And that whatever I forgot to do for them—to teach, show, notice, praise, give, or honor—they must do for themselves, or else do without. And that was why I could not sleep. ("Whose Life Is It Anyway?" Good Housekeeping, February 1994, p. 62, excerpt from I'm Still Your Mother: How to Get Along with Your Grown-Up Children for the Rest of Your Life, New York: Delacorte Press, 1994.)

With all of these changes and feelings, the confusion and ambivalence, what can parents do? How can we make it through this passage positively and successfully, retaining our sanity and not alienating our kids?

HOW TO RESPOND

1. Accept the Realities

Recovery groups have long used a version of Reinhold Niebuhr's Serenity Prayer: "God grant me the serenity to accept the things I cannot change, the courage to change the things I can, and the wisdom to know the difference." This prayer has profound implications for parents, especially during this crucial passage. By nature we resist change, especially when things are going well. Change makes us nervous and insecure. Yet during this passage our family, our high school graduates, and our parent-child relationships are changing considerably.

Some changes we need to accept—so we need serenity. Some changes we need to make—so we need courage. But most of all, we need wisdom to know the difference.

Release

Perhaps the biggest change concerns the fact that your child has crossed the threshold into adulthood. They are no longer your little boy or girl. Having the *serenity* to accept this truth means releasing your child from your grasp. Stu Weber writes:

> *One of the things we need to restore is a sense of release, a moment in time when everybody involved in our child's life realizes, "This young person is now responsible for their own life." That can come in any number of ways. With my own parents, it wasn't a formal event at all. It was a moment none of us would have or could have rehearsed. I don't know how deliberate or practiced it was, but I do remember it as vividly now as the day it happened. It took place at a train depot. I was off for college. For the first time in my life I was leaving home for an extended season. I saw it in their eyes. It was strong. It was an unforgettable moment. In later years, my mother would say that from that moment on, it was never the same. It was more than getting on a train for Illinois. It was leaving childhood. (Tender Warrior: God's Intention for a Man, Sisters, Oreg.: Multnomah, 1993, p. 166)*

In Jesus' parable of the Prodigal Son, recorded in Luke

15:11-32, the father released his younger son to take his inheritance early and set off on his own. The father didn't kick his son out of the house or abandon him, and he didn't angrily announce, "Go ahead, mess up your life! But don't come running back here when you're broke and desperate!" The loving father allowed his son to leave, to live far away, and to squander his fortune. But all the while the father was waiting, scanning the horizon for his son, ready to welcome him home. When the son finally returned, the father didn't question his appearance or greet him with an "I told you so" speech. No, he "was filled with compassion for him; he ran to his son, threw his arms around him and kissed him" (Luke 15:20, NIV), and he threw a party! That's what it means to *release*, to let go.

It's fun to relate to my kids as friends—adult to adult.

Paul Veerman

Even though it will be difficult, you need to turn the corner mentally and agree with your children that they are now adults and largely responsible for their own lives.

Forgive

Another important aspect of accepting present realities is to set aside the past. Both you and your child have made mistakes, spoken hateful words, and chosen wrong directions. But that is in the past—let it go. This is the opportunity to make a fresh start.

Some parents use the past as a weapon, constantly reminding children of their mistakes:

- I told you to take biology; now you'll never get into premed.
- Just think, you could have married Michael—look what he's done with his life!
- When I think of those wasted years in high school, I just want to cry.
- If you had worked harder and hustled more, you could have had that scholarship.

And some parents beat themselves with the past, constantly reviewing and reliving crucial moments or lost opportunities.

Pray as did David: "Create in me a new, clean heart, O God, filled with clean thoughts and right desires. . . . Restore to me again the joy of your salvation, and make me willing to obey you" (Psalm 51:10, 12, TLB). Then let it go. Forgive yourself and your child. Move on.

Bless

Accepting this change in your child's life also means giving them your blessing.

I'll never forget when Mom and Dad left me at college. We had said our good-byes—I had kissed Mom and had shaken Dad's hand. Then, just before Dad got into the car, he looked me in the eye and, choking back the tears, said, "Thanks for being such a good son and for being a good example for your brothers and sister." It wasn't much—just a short sentence—but it meant the world to me. Dad was giving me his blessing and telling me that I was moving into a new era in my life. More than three decades later, I read the following in his reflections: *When it became obvious to me that Ralph and Paul were following the same pattern as Dave, I made a point of telling Dave how much I appreciated the good example he set for his brothers—and I meant every word.*

About six months into his life in the military, during an otherwise mundane phone conversation, my son floored me with the simple question, "So how are *you* doing, Dad?" The hint of peer caring caught me by surprise. Matt was beginning to see that his father was someone who might not be doing all right and probably ought to be asked once in a while to make sure. What I tried to do was thank him for asking. I didn't know what else to say. But when I hung up the phone, I wept. We really don't understand how deep our need to be cared for by our children runs until they reveal it by caring. We never stop needing each other. The opportunities to express our needs and meet each other's needs may change throughout life, but the needs will always be there.

Neil Wilson

Be sure to give your sons and daughters your blessing, telling them of your approval, saying how proud you are, and reassuring them of your love. You should do this in person, privately, one-on-one, but you can reaffirm your statement on the phone and through cards and letters. Gail is terrific at this. Remembering how much college students love to get mail, she sends Kara cards from time to time. Inside each one she will jot a brief note expressing her joy at having such a wonderful daughter, reminding her of our love, and promising to pray for her. Kara has often expressed how much these little notes mean to her.

2. Roll with the Changes

Earlier we looked at the changes to the parents, the family structure, and the young person. When these changes occur, you have a choice: You can resist them or roll with them. Resisting will usually create conflict and drive your child away emotionally as well as physically. But rolling with the changes—accepting and adapting to them—will keep the communication lines open and help build a stronger relationship between you and your young adult.

Family Structure

The change in family structure becomes obvious during the late adolescent's first visit home.

I am the oldest of five children. The next in line is my brother Ralph, two and a half years younger than I. Although we had our typical sibling battles, Ralph and I have always been very close. In fact, when I went off to college, I could tell that he was very proud of me and almost idolized me. I remember getting letters from Ralph at football camp and during the first couple of months of school. When I went home at Thanksgiving, however, I sensed a tension between us, as though he resented me being there. Then I realized what was happening. With my vacancy, Ralph had moved up in the sibling pecking order—he was now the oldest child at home, the senior member of the troop, and clearly enjoying that position. I returned, expecting things to be as they had been, but the family dynamic had changed. Ralph was fifteen and beginning to make a name for himself in high school. He was asserting himself in the family and receiving a lot of attention from Mom and Dad. I was a threat to his new role. I quickly realized that I had to back off and act more like a guest than a big brother. Things had changed.

In a smaller family, that change won't be quite so obvious, but it is there nonetheless. With Kara gone, Dana quite naturally receives nearly all of our attention. Now our family schedule revolves, for the most part, around her and her activities.

Family Rules

Another change relates to family rules and discipline. A college-professor friend explained that he warns all his freshmen advisees about their first trip home: *Here at the university, you can come and go as you please and set your own curfew.*

226

It's been nice—you have enjoyed your freedom. But when you go home, you will be directly under your parents' authority again and living by their rules. It will feel different, and you probably won't like it.

If you've been on a college campus lately, you've probably noticed that many of the social events begin after 10 P.M. About the time that you normally go to bed, they're just getting wound up. Have you tried calling a college student? Many don't get to their rooms until midnight. The other day my nephew, a college junior, told me that his intramural basketball game was scheduled for 10:30, and that was on a Tuesday night! Typical college students stay up late, sleep in when they can, and sometimes run for days on latent energy. Whether it's studying, playing sports or cards, ordering a pizza and talking with friends, going on a date, or just messing around, the late-night hours are usually used for everything except sleep.

Contrast this with the student's former life in high school. Because every day the class schedule was the same, the regular routine demanded no late activities on *school nights*. On weekends, the schedule was relaxed, but still the curfew was at midnight.

Now put the high school and college schedules together—they don't match at all! And if you try to make them match, you'll have a problem.

Often it happens like this: Trent comes home from college for Christmas vacation, but he's rarely there. Instead, he's at Bob's or Jack's or shooting baskets at the Y or meeting friends at the show. Mom and Dad want to spend time with Trent, but they don't see him. They hear him come in at about 2 A.M., and they see him sleeping when they get up and leave each morning. He's living like a college student, and they're living as they always have. Things have changed.

To roll with change, you should talk with your child and explain the differences without condescending or putting them down. Explain that you understand that they have grown beyond high school and hasn't been living under high school rules and regulations. Then discuss what a realistic curfew would be, considering the student's freedom and being considerate of the other family members. Also discuss when the whole family could do activities together. Come to a mutual understanding of the house rules and the penalties for disobeying them.

I am not advocating total abdication of parental authority and responsibility. You will always be the parent, and your child should honor and respect you as such. As the parent, it is your responsibility to care for your family and run your household. You wouldn't allow a house guest to do anything he pleased; why should you allow your own child? Just remember, however, that your authority over your child is changing. And if everything goes right, soon they will be totally on their own and completely out from under your authority and supervision.

Ideas and Concepts

Another change is the emergence of your child's ability to think analytically and critically, especially if they are in college. In college classes, students are expected to doubt and test various theories and points of view, to think through the issues, and to arrive at their own conclusions. Learning to analyze and have informed opinions can be painful for both the student and parents.

There's nothing more frustrating for parents than a son discovering his mind or a daughter who has had one psychology or philosophy course and thinks that she has everything figured out. I remember coming home from college and arguing with my mother about racial prejudice, politics, and theology. I was learning to think on my own, to form my own opinions . . . and I was obnoxious.

When I was a boy of fourteen, my father was so ignorant I could hardly stand to have the old man around. But when I got to be twenty-one, I was astonished at how much the old man had learned in seven years.

Mark Twain

When this happens, when your student makes an inflammatory remark or spouts the latest psychobabble, do your best to listen quietly and respectfully and try not to get into an argument. Bruce Barton advises that a parent's first response be positive, saying something like, "That's interesting." Look for something positive to affirm and let your child know that you respect their opinion. Then give a few thoughts, facts, and ideas on the other side of the argument for them *to think about.* I'm sure my parents must have wondered what my professors were teaching me in college. But they patiently allowed me to think and to work through my ideas, and we kept a close relationship.

One woman told me that she would always come home with extremely liberal ideas, echoing her professors at the university. She and her father would argue, but he never got upset with her. He simply would counter with conservative answers and cause her to think through her position.

Personal Faith

The process of learning how to think can also cause many conflicts in Christian homes as students begin to question their faith.

I had been reared in a wonderful Christian home and had been heavily involved in a strong evangelical church. In fact, at times I was more zealous in my *witnessing* and *separation from the world* than either my parents or the church had promoted. I had made a profession of faith in Christ as my personal Savior when I was seven years old (my mother prayed with me after a Child Evangelism Fellowship meeting in our home) and had been immersed in church activities all my life. So I thought I had all the answers when I left for college. But there I encountered students much more devoted to Christ than I who believed differently in some areas. From other students and in various classes, I heard questions for which I had no answers. And what was even more disconcerting, I discovered that I had answers for questions that no one was asking.

Suddenly my faith began to seem irrelevant and childish, and I began to struggle with doubts. I had been an *environmental Christian.* My Christianity had come from my environment, had been given to me by others; it wasn't my own. So when I had left my home and Christian environment, in effect I had left my faith. I doubted everything: the truth of the Bible, Jesus Christ as divine, and even the existence of God. But through the next couple of years and by the grace of God and help of dedicated Christian professors and friends, I was able to believe again, but this time my faith was my own!

Those who work with university students say that most kids, even at Christian schools, don't attend church much during their freshman year. So if your child sleeps in or studies on Sunday mornings, don't panic—such behavior is typical.

Parents who send kids to Christian schools often think that the environment at the schools will protect their children and encourage them to grow spiritually. Parents who see their kids go off on their own, enlist in the military, or go to a secular university often worry that their children will be pressured and tempted to deny their faith and abandon their morals. In *both* situations, anything is possible because the young person is away from home and free to make their own choices. If your child moves to a Christian environment, don't be lulled into complacency, thinking that they won't be challenged or tempted. If your child moves to a secular environment, don't be worried sick that they will wipe out theologically and morally. Pray and trust God.

Your child is in his hands, as Jeremiah declared: "O Lord God! You have made the heavens and earth by your great power; nothing is too hard for you!" (Jeremiah 32:17, TLB).

Mitzie Barton explains that she prayed daily that Kari would find a Christian friend at her secular all-women school. When that didn't happen the first year, Mitzie decided that God would answer her prayer in his way and in his time, and she kept praying. The next year, the university hired a new basketball coach—a dedicated Christian woman. Mitzie says, "At that school, that was a miracle and a sure sign that God was taking care of my daughter."

Pray that your child connects with a strong Christian friend, coach, teacher, or small group.

Because your sons and daughters are maturing, they will change in the spiritual area. When changes begin to occur, there's not much you can do except rely on God and encourage them to be honest seekers in their search for the truth. They may want to try other churches. Often kids from liturgical backgrounds will begin attending Baptist, Assembly of God, or Bible churches and exclaim that the services are so *free* and the people so friendly. Conversely, young people from informal worship settings will often gravitate to Lutheran, Episcopal, or Roman Catholic churches and remark that the services are so *worshipful.* That's all part of the process of personalizing faith, making it their own.

Remember, too, that if you've done a good job in teaching Christian values and in building a solid faith foundation, your child won't throw everything overboard and join a cult. I know that my girls are much better prepared to build their faith and deal with doubt because of the outstanding youth ministry at our church. They were exposed to C. S. Lewis and other strong Christian thinkers whom I didn't discover until college.

Roll with these changes and trust God for the outcome.

3. Treat Your Child like a Friend

Because your child is maturing and quickly becoming an adult, you now have an excellent opportunity to move toward a peer relationship. You will always be the parent, but you can also be a friend.

Activities

When your maturing children are home on vacation or military leave, look for activities that they would enjoy—adult activities such as going out for lunch, shopping, attending a professional sporting event, and so forth. I have seen men bring their college-age sons to men's breakfasts and retreats, and I've seen women bring their daughters to Bible studies and luncheons. At church, take your child with you to an adult class. In other words, help your graduate move away from the high school world and into the adult world.

Discussions

Another way to treat your maturing children like friends is to ask for their opinion. Years ago, a good friend told me, "I will learn from you if I think you can learn from me." His point was that peer communication is a two-way street. In friendship, one person doesn't dominate, speak down to the other, or have all the answers. Friends treat each other as equals, each with something significant to contribute.

Think of how you might be able to get your child involved in your life. What question could you ask? What problem could you pose? Don't make one up—ask a legitimate question for which you need an answer. And when your child responds, listen carefully and take their answer seriously.

Also, work at crafting thoughtful questions that you can ask about your child's life away from home. Don't ask questions that can be answered with yes, no, or another one-word response. For example, instead of asking, "How was school?" or "How's the job going?" you could ask, "What have you been discussing in your sociology class lately?" or "What evidence do you see at work that the economy is improving?" Thoughtful questions treat your child as an adult and aren't perceived as intrusive.

Get into the habit of talking things over with your nearly adult child. Your children don't have to be home for these discussions; you can make a phone call or write a letter. Invite them into your life.

Sharing

Friends share experiences. Look for opportunities to do something together that will give you something to talk about. For example, you could rent a thought-provoking video and watch it together. You could attend a political rally or a public lecture. You could read the same book.

Of course you don't have to do something serious. You could work out, play golf, fish, or go to a comedy club. Choose an activity that you can talk during and about. The goal is to find something you can do together.

Having children graduate from high school and leave home can be a difficult passage as parents' emotions run the gamut: joy, fear, hope, and grief. You can work through this passage and help your late adolescent move toward maturity by *accepting the realities, rolling with the changes,* and *treating them like a friend.*

LET'S THINK ABOUT IT

Warnings
- *Don't treat your young adults like children.* They are growing up. Help your sons and daughters grow.
- *Don't expect things at home to be the same as before your child left.* The family structure and dynamics will change.
- *Don't argue with your college student's new theories and ideas.* Your maturing children are learning to analyze and to express concepts and opinions. Affirm what is positive in their declarations and statements.

Opportunities
- *You can build a friendship with your late adolescents.* They are becoming adults like you.
- *You can bless your children* with loving affirmation as you send them off to college, the military, or employment.

- *You can rejoice in what God has done through you in your sons and daughters.* They have made it through the tough junior high and senior high years and are doing well.
- *You can help your sons and daughters grow spiritually as they personalize Christianity.* Take their questions seriously and encourage them to look for answers and make the faith their own.

Lessons

- *Change is often painful, but it is necessary for our child's growth.* If we've done our job right as parents, eventually we will come to the day when our children will leave us. We grieve the loss, but that's the way it should be, and that's what we want.
- *Change gives us the chance to grow* as we evaluate our lives, our relationship with our children, and our relationship with God. Eventually, we have to release each child, to allow them to live independently, apart from us, just as we were released by our parents.

Resources

- Doug and Ron Hutchcraft, *Letters from the College Front—Boys' Edition* (Grand Rapids: Baker, 1993). This book and the companion volume for girls give down-to-earth advice for surviving and thriving in college. Written in a letters-to-home style, the books are easy to read and are ideal for high school juniors and seniors and college freshmen.

◆ Jerry B. Jenkins, *As You Leave Home* (Colorado Springs: Focus on the Family, 1993). This is a refreshingly honest message to a son as he embarks on his life away from home and his parents. Packed with emotion, Jerry also shares invaluable advice on becoming a man, building solid values, and keeping close to God.

Giving
Them Away

9

Wedding Checklist—Parents of the Bride

___ *Meet future son-in-law*

___ *Give him "the speech"*

___ *Give approval/blessing for marriage*

___ *Breathe sigh of relief*

____ *Discuss wedding plans with daughter*

____ *Work out budget*

____ *Apply for loan*

____ *Try to convince daughter to elope*

____ *Make wedding arrangements*

____ *Veto "Sunrise, Sunset" solo*

____ *Practice smile for wedding pictures*

____ *Practice saying "Her mother and I"*

____ *Finally get around to giving her "the talk"*

____ *Butt out of the wedding plans*

Wedding Checklist—Parents of the Groom

____ *Talk with son about this big step*

____ *Meet future daughter-in-law*

____ *Act thrilled*

____ *Give them "the speech"*

____ *Ask about wedding plans*

____ *Give bride invitation list (be ready to defend)*

____ *Suppress anxiety over son's ability to provide*

____ *Make travel arrangements*

_____ *Apply for loan*

_____ *Practice meeting her parents*

_____ *Finally get around to giving him "the talk"*

_____ *Butt out of the wedding plans*

Do you remember when you decided to get married? Undoubtedly it was a time of mixed feelings. You were excited about making this lifetime commitment to the one you loved so dearly. Yet you probably harbored a few doubts and had anxious moments when you considered the full impact of what you were going to do.

Remember the week before the wedding? Those nagging doubts may have increased as the tension of preparing for the wedding mounted. Yet you rushed toward that day, carried by love, the well-wishes of close friends and relatives, and the wedding preparations themselves.

Do you remember the wedding ceremony? Seeing your bride or groom standing there, smiling broadly, you knew it was right, but it felt like a dream or a play. You probably can't recall much of the ceremony, except the introduction as "Mr. and Mrs." and then the quick walk down the aisle together.

And what do you remember of the reception and the getaway? Do you remember your father's last words of advice, your mother's tears, and their good-bye hugs? What do you think they were feeling as you drove off to the honeymoon? Because the whole event was centered around you, you probably don't remember much about your parents, individually and as a couple. I know I don't. In fact, the whole day seems like a blur in my memory. I remember more about the honeymoon.

Now, as parents, we are on the other side of the wedding. And we are very aware of our feelings and actions as we approach the event—an important day in our child's life and a crucial passage in our parenting adventure.

Emotions permeate this ninth passage, as with the others. These emotions can catch us by surprise, especially since we were oblivious to what our parents were feeling when we got married. The emotions are similar to those felt during the last passage, when our children left home. It is another time of letting go and of feeling the loss.

MIXED EMOTIONS

In this passage, even more than the others, parents' emotions are mixed. Of course, the mixture and depth of feelings vary greatly depending on family circumstances and the individuals involved. Many relationship variables affect the equation. Regardless of the situation, however, all families find this passage emotionally charged.

Anger

Some parents react with anger at the news of their child's wedding plans. Perhaps they don't like the boyfriend or girlfriend, or maybe they think their child is too young or immature to get married. Others may be angry because the relationship with their child is already strained—getting married is a way for the child to hurt the parents, to strike back, to demonstrate independence. Some parents focus their anger on the girlfriend or boyfriend, thinking that they are trying to steal their child away.

An overused plot of television dramas involves a mother or father threatening to disown the child or cut them out of the will because of an impending marriage. Whether or not those fictional accounts are true to life, we do know of many weddings that were rushed, ill-advised, and motivated by a desire for sex, money, or revenge.

Parents also may react with anger because they have not navigated successfully through their previous parenting passages.

A couple found it difficult to grant any independence to their son in middle and late adolescence and have tried to run his life several years after high school graduation. Marriage is a blow to their control.

A mother dreamed of a specific career path for her daughter and hasn't accepted her daughter's different desires. She truly believes that this young man, her daughter's boyfriend, is thwarting her and turning her daughter against her. Marriage is killing her dream.

A father sees his son's desires turning toward a young woman and away from the athletic field. Marriage is hurting his ego.

I know of a woman who was dead set against her daughter's marriage because she wanted her daughter to continue her education and eventually earn her doctorate. Although the daughter and her fiancé were college graduates and strong Christians, this mother fought them at every step and was furious at the young man for detouring her daughter from advanced education. This mother of the bride came to the wedding, but wore black and refused to be included in any pictures. Only when her first grandchild was born did she begin to warm to her son-in-law.

Whatever the cause of the anger, it's not worth dividing parents from their children. These moms and dads should seek counseling and take actions that will result in reconciliation and healing.

Beyond dysfunctional families and irrational anger, even parents in healthy parent-child relationships feel conflicting emotions.

Excitement/Dread

When parents hear their child's declaration of love and intention to marry, the usual response is excitement.

Listening to a daughter gush over *Mr. Wonderful* or a son talk nonstop about this terrific girl, we can't help but be enthusiastic—it's contagious. Watching and hearing them talk with great animation about the person with whom they are in love reminds us of when they were children, opening gifts on Christmas morning or delighting in the amusement park. We love seeing our children happy.

In most pending marriages, the parents have already met the person that their child is planning to marry and have gotten used to the idea of having them around. So they are excited about the progression of the relationship and the prospect of having a new member of the family. Lew and Dottye Luttrell explain that when the kids were quite young, they began praying for the man and woman Jennifer and Kirk would eventually marry. Dottye says, "I was so excited to meet Cliff. I had prayed for him, her future husband, for so long." Lew adds, "And as soon as we met Ann, we were sure that she was the one."

━━━━━━━━━━━━━━━━━━━━━━━━━━━

Giving away my daughter in marriage was like giving a priceless Stradivarius violin to a gorilla.

Bufe Karraker

━━━━━━━━━━━━━━━━━━━━━━━━━━━

Don and Lorna Ray explain that they were excited at their son Bill's wedding because they thought Bill and Sarah were ready to get married. In fact, they thought Bill was going too slow in the process. *We wanted Bill to propose and get on with it. He was old enough and mature enough, and we thought the world of Sarah. We certainly didn't want him to keep living at home. And we were happy with the direction they were going. So we were excited when Bill finally proposed and they set the date.*

Excitement also builds about the event itself. Weddings are family reunions—wonderful reasons for family and friends to gather, reminisce, and celebrate. Although it will be expensive, we want the very best for our children and don't mind paying the money (within reason, of course). And let's be honest: A wedding is a great excuse to have a terrific party!

As the wedding day approaches, however, parents may

experience a growing sense of dread, knowing that the wedding vows are also a public declaration of independence from them. At every passage since sending them to school, we have had to let loose a bit, allowing our children to mature into thinking, self-disciplined, and self-reliant adults. But through it all and underneath it all, we still have been in control (unless the child has been away from home and on their own for a few years).

During high school, we still fed, clothed, and housed our children. After graduation we paid some of the bills and gave the kids a refuge and a place to come home. In all these situations, regardless of the freedom we granted our sons and daughters, we still had a measure of control and close influence in their lives. But marriage is a public signal that they are moving out and on their own, establishing their own homes and families.

Don Ray admits that, as Donna prepared for her wedding, he felt a lot of pangs about losing his daughter. "I thought I would do things differently, but I lost control and didn't handle my emotions well at all. I guess it was a father-daughter thing."

We're excited about the wedding and what it means for our young adults, but there's a part of every parent that dreads the day that they leave home forever.

Hope/Worry

What's your favorite wedding story? I have witnessed or heard of soloists forgetting their words, of writing on the soles of the groom's shoes, and of fainting, open flies, young children's comments, late brides, rolling rings, and many other humorous events. In each case, however, the audience laughed and the ceremony continued. It is virtually impossible to ruin a wedding with a miscue, gaffe, or mild practical joke. At such a happy occasion, everyone is forgiving. Celebrating the beginning of a couple's life together, weddings focus on the future and are filled with hope. Talk at the reception centers around the beauty of the bride, the lovely ceremony, and the couple's plans for the future. Hope fills the entire celebration.

Hope also permeates the service. I have performed several weddings and have been a participant or guest at dozens of others. I always get a chuckle out of some of the elements of the ceremonies, especially when the bride and groom each take a lit candle, light a single candle in the middle of the two, and then extinguish their individual candles, symbolizing two lives becoming one. Knowing that marriage takes work and can be a struggle, I wonder if two or three years later the couple would feel the same about the candle routine. Perhaps they would find another way to use the candles to illustrate the realities of marriage and the difficulty of truly *becoming one.*

Christian marriage is the ultimate merger. It calls two different persons to blend into a unique mixture without losing their identities. No forcing a square peg into a round hole, pinching one and pulling another. Rather, God planted a magnet inside His creatures. One shares another without losing oneness. Two bond into a unit without two-ness. The Bible calls it a mystery. We may describe some of its parts; we can only experience its fullness. . . .

Howard and Jeanne Hendricks, Husbands and Wives (Wheaton, Ill.: Victor, 1988), p. 15.

Weddings also overflow with idealism. Consider the vows of lifelong commitment to each other, no matter what happens. I don't believe anyone goes into a marriage expecting to divorce in a few months or years. At most weddings the couple commits to a lifetime together, and they really expect it. Listen carefully to the vows. Whether they write their own or repeat the ones in the minister's manual, the young man and woman make incredible promises to each other. At our wedding rehearsal, when the minister said, "For better or worse, richer or poorer, in sickness or in health . . . ," Gail responded, "I'll take better, rich, and healthy." The minister laughed and reminded us that it wasn't multiple choice. But regardless of what they promise, most couples expect a bliss-filled, trouble-free life together.

This idealism causes us to mix worry with our hope. We know that marriages and families are under enormous stress in our society these days. In fact, it has become increasingly difficult to stay married. These days, more than half of all marriages end in divorce, and it's not unusual for a person to be married three or four times. Living together has become socially acceptable, and promiscuity is viewed by many as the normal lifestyle for healthy singles. Sex sells products, and people sell sex. Marital fidelity is dismissed by many as old-fashioned.

Love American-style suggests that a person should find someone to love, which is interpreted as someone who makes them feel good and who meets all their needs. Because contemporary love is self-centered and based on feelings, young men and women flock to the altar, make their pledges of undying love, and then run from the marriages as soon as the feelings fade or personal needs change.

Many years ago, parents arranged their children's marriages. The kids didn't first fall in love and then decide to marry; they had to learn to love the individuals they married. Certainly we would not want to return to the days of arranged marriages. But we must realize that, no matter what the dating-engagement-wedding routine, every married person still has to learn to love the person that they have married.

The attacks on marriage cause us to wonder how our children will fare . . . and we worry.

We also worry because we know that love hurts and that marriage takes work. It's easy to intone "for better or worse, richer or poorer, in sickness or in health," but most husbands and wives turn out to be worse than expected—we're human, sinful, and self-centered. Before the wedding, Gail and I knew each other pretty well, but I was shocked at what I learned about myself afterward. I didn't know I could be so hateful and treat Gail so terribly. I am sure I was worse than she expected.

My Dear Karen,

Many couples make the mistake of thinking that two saying "I do!" means "We did it!" They assume that by the mere act of climbing the chancel steps they have already vaulted the stairs into heaven. . . .

Marriage may be "made in heaven" in the original. But the whole deal is more like one of those kits which comes knocked down for putting together. It will take some gluing here, sanding rough spots there, hammering a bit now, filing down the scratches on this side, planing a bit on that side, carving a piece, bending this section slightly, varnishing, backing off for a frequent look, dusting, waxing, polishing, until at last what you have is a thing of beauty and a joy forever.

Charlie Shedd, Letters to Karen (Nashville: Abingdon, 1965), p. 25.

Most young married couples struggle financially. During the engagement and at the altar, money doesn't seem very important. After the wedding, however, reality sets in as the bills mount up. Many couples work long hours at two jobs so that someday they will fulfill the American dream: a home of their own loaded with all the modern appliances, two cars in the garage, two kids, a sizable bank account, full-coverage health insurance, and a retirement stash. Money causes most of the arguments in marriages. We may want *richer,* but usually we get *poorer.*

What about *in sickness or in health?* Besides colds, flu, toothaches, and other common aches and pains, every home experiences severe health problems—it is part of being human. In our twenty-five years of marriage, I've had three bouts with kidney stones, two episodes of severe back pain, a cracked rib, encephalitis, and migraine headaches—and I consider myself to be very healthy.

Physical deterioration is a part of growing older. I remember whispering romantically to Gail, "Let's grow old together." But have you visited a nursing home lately? Old is not fun. My mother died of Alzheimer's disease. She had begun to show symptoms in her sixties—she died at seventy-four. My father died two years earlier of congestive heart failure as he tried to care for Mom. He was true to his commitment of October 18, 1941 and stayed by her *in sickness.*

We know those realities. So while we smile at the young couple's idealism and offer our sincere congratulations and best wishes, we also worry about how they will react during the tough times. We hope for the very best, but we also worry.

Joy/Sorrow

Our third combination of emotions is the mix of joy and sorrow. Nelson Bennett confesses: *Leading up to our son's wedding, I was fine. In fact, I would joke that we were "losing a tax deduction but gaining a daughter." And because Theo and Carol Joy were moving to New Mexico, I talked about them being our "meal ticket" to the Southwest. I thought that if anyone got emotional, it would be Marcee. But during the ceremony, I lost it completely. I cried tears of joy—I was thrilled with the occasion and what God was doing in my son's life. But I also felt lost and an overwhelming sense of loss.*

We rejoice because this is what we have dreamed for our sons and daughters when they were young: to grow, mature, follow Christ, find the right persons to marry, establish their own homes, and have Christian families. The wedding isn't the end of the process, but it is a significant step in the right direction. So we proudly stand in the receiving line, accept congratulations and hugs, smile continuously, and thank God for his goodness.

Our joy is heightened when we know and love the young man or woman our child will marry. I've spoken with many parents whose children have married wonderful Christian young men and women. Understandably, these moms and dads are thrilled—and they give me hope for my daughters.

As with many of the other parenting passages, our joy is tempered by sorrow. Parents cry at weddings not just because they are happy but also because they are grieving the passing of childhood. Mom and Dad acknowledge and accept their child's declaration of independence, but it is sad just the same.

Mark Senter reports that after his daughter Jori's wedding, he stood with her father-in-law and watched the happy couple drive away. This man had already married off four other children. Mark turned to speak to him, but the father couldn't even talk, he was so choked with emotion. Mark said, "It's tough, isn't it?" And all he could answer was, "Yeah!" His last little boy had grown up.

Amid the joy of the marriage, we also face the reality that the child may soon move far away. For many years, my brothers, sister, and I lived in the Midwest, at the most a few hours from each other and Mom and Dad. But our family was the exception. Many of the young couples I knew lived several states away from at least one set of parents. Then it happened to us: In one year, Ralph moved to Washington, Paul moved to Connecticut, and I moved to Louisiana. Our close family was spread across the country. I often wondered how Mom and Dad felt about us suddenly being so many miles away.

Lorna Ray shares what most parents probably feel: "We moved away when we got married, but we don't want our kids to do that. We want them close."

In this extremely mobile society, however, moving has become a fact of life. It's not unusual for a family's children to be spread all over the world. It is very unlikely that the parents of *both* the husband and wife will live in the same community.

The most overwhelming feeling, however, is sorrow that the child has really grown up. Beyond the symbol of independence, the reality is that they are not the little boy or little girl anymore. This truth hits some parents long before the wedding as they begin to make the preparations. Others don't think about it until they hear their child repeat their vows.

Jim Green performed the wedding ceremonies for his daughters, Jana and Jarin. Jim says that he had a tough time during Jana's wedding because every time he looked at her, everything he said brought a flood of memories from her childhood. He was better prepared for Jarin's wedding because he knew what to expect, but still there were emotional moments during the ceremony.

For some, like Mark Senter, it is a delayed reaction. Continuing with his story about Jori's wedding, Mark explains that everything about the wedding day was absolutely wonderful, and it all went smoothly. Before bed that night, he and Ruth talked with their son Nick about how great the wedding was. Then they all went to bed. Mark says: *Ruth went to sleep, but I just lay there and looked at the ceiling. Suddenly it hit me that I didn't have a little girl anymore. I didn't sleep much that night, so I got up early and started writing in my journal. I couldn't stop crying. They were tears of joy, but also of sorrow. In the middle of my journaling, the phone rang. It was Jori. (She had said that she would call us in the morning.) She sensed right away that something was wrong and asked, "Are you OK?" I chose to be honest and replied softly, "I have just been writing that I've lost my little girl." Then I paused, composed myself, and continued, "But it's OK . . . and so am I." Then we were able to have a great talk about the wedding and their honeymoon plans.*

For Nelson Bennett, the feelings continued and seemed to come in waves: *The day after Theo was married, we were packing up his van, and I broke down again. As we were walking away, I let him know what I was feeling—how hard it was for me, but how glad I was for him. Recently, when Theo and Carol were in town for Christmas, we had a great time together. But it was really tough when they had to leave.*

*I probably sound overly dramatic, but I felt a sense of loss, finality. I thought, "My son is **gone**. My life will be different."*

A wedding can be a sad occasion as parents recognize that their boy or girl isn't little anymore and that soon they won't see their child very often.

No matter how close the bride-to-be was with her fiancé's family, as a wife, she may have trouble getting along with her husband's mother. And even if she supported her husband's choice of a career before they were married, she may still fight against it afterward. In both cases she is simply feeling threatened by anything that competes for her husband's loyalty and affection.

Men—don't take it personally and defend your mother or your job. Let your wife know that you have *left home* and that she has a higher priority in your life.

Moms—don't take it personally when your daughter-in-law seems cold and distant. Keep loving and praying for her and the marriage. With a little time and the confidence that she has your son's love, she will warm up to you.

Dave Veerman

These mixed emotions can surprise and confuse us, and they can pull us in many directions. But they can also balance us out and help us through this passage. Our dread can be alleviated by the excitement of preparing for the glorious event. Those who might tend to be overly anxious and consumed by worry can be encouraged by hope. And parents' sorrow can be overcome by the joy of seeing the fruit of trusting God and rearing kids by following godly principles. But how should we respond to help our sons and daughters during this passage of parenting?

HOW TO RESPOND

Because the feelings during this passage are similar to our emotions when children leave home, our actions will also have some similarities.

1. Let Go

In Eden God said, "It is not good for the man to be alone" (Genesis 2:18, NIV), so he created Eve and brought her to Adam. Then the Bible says, "For this reason a man will leave his father and mother and be united to his wife, and they will become one flesh" (Genesis 2:24, NIV). In a discussion with the Pharisees about marriage and divorce, Jesus quoted this verse (Matthew 19:5). Paul used the same quote in his letter to the Ephesians (Ephesians 5:31). It is clearly an important statement on marriage.

The statement has three verbs, three actions that a marriage couple are to take: *will leave, be united,* and *will become.* The first, *will leave,* implies a movement away from home. Clearly when a man and woman marry, they must first leave their homes and families in order to build their own. This leaving is more than simply living in another house. It means leaving emotionally as well as physically. The son and daughter must truly leave home and become independent of their parents. In fact, they cannot *be united* fully unless they really leave.

Giving a Push

But sometimes the child does not want to leave. Even though they go through the wedding ceremony and pledge total commitment to their partner, they still have not let go of Father's hand or Mother's apron strings. That's when Mom and Dad have to exercise tough love, firmly but tenderly insisting that their child grow up, make their own decisions, and become the husband or wife that God intended.

In *As You Leave Home,* Jerry Jenkins gives his son this wise, but tough, counsel:

> *If it insults you that I feel the need to remind you that you are now on your own, forgive me. The second to the last thing I want you to picture in your mind is that the shut door I just mentioned is also locked. (The last is that I'm here to make your life easier.)*
>
> *I make that careful distinction because the day may come when life defeats you. If you are injured or ill to the point that you can't function, I am still your parent, we are still your family. If you fail so miserably that your options are gone and you can't go on, by all means know that here, with me, you have a refuge.*
>
> *You may be so bitterly disappointed or grieving that you simply need to know someone is behind you. Never doubt it. If you lose a spouse, a child, or a home, you are still part*

of this family. You may have left and cleaved to someone else, but you still have a refuge.

In case you're wondering how serious things have to become before you should look this way, try these on for size:

If your course load is too heavy, don't come running home.

If you have procrastinated to the point where you will fail no matter how hard you work, don't come running home.

If you have come to loggerheads with your spouse, and understanding and communication are gone, don't come running home.

Stay in the game. Work at it, study it, plan for it, pray it through. You're on your own. You're building muscle. You're becoming a person who will one day train another to become independent. (Colorado Springs: Focus on the Family, 1993, pp. 16–17)

You may have to insist that your child *leave* and grow up. This can be as hard on you, the parent, as on your child.

Releasing Your Grip

Often the opposite occurs—a bride's or groom's leaving is hindered by the parents. Hating to see their baby grow up (or denying they *have*), they continue to treat their child as though the individual were still in college or high school. I've heard of cases where the mother takes meals to the couple, does their laundry, and calls every day, attempting to keep her child close to home. In extreme cases such as those, the couple may have to move a few hours away in order to find space and make their own lives.

On this whole issue of letting go, I need to add a note for parents whose children are adults and still single. A wedding ceremony is a clear sign that this passage into adulthood has occurred for the child, but with older, single children, that passage is not so clear. Thus many parents continue to interfere in their older children's lives. We need to come to the point where we realize that they truly are grown-up and on their own.

When Art and Carol Wittmann's daughter got married, they experienced a different twist in this whole issue of letting go. They had "released their grip" on Heather when she married Tom, and Carol and Heather had grown close, as good friends. But as Carol explains: *I was still her mother. When Heather and Tom were going through some tough times in their marriage, I got too emotionally involved. The kind of things she would share were too close to me, so I would react as a mother to what Heather would tell me. Then I became the bad guy. I finally told her, "We can be good friends, but I can't be your best friend. You need to find someone else." I still need to be there for her to call if things aren't going well, but she can't use me as her sounding board. I decided that Heather and Tom needed to work things out on their own and that we had intervened too far. We were trying to control the situation.*

Art adds: *We can't live Heather's life—she has to do it. Now I can see the truth of Romans 5:3-5: "We also rejoice in our sufferings, because we know that suffering produces perseverance; perseverance, character; and character, hope. And hope does not disappoint us, because God has poured out his love into our hearts by the Holy Spirit, whom he has given us"* (NIV).

Although it is painful, we have to let go completely, giving up our control and allowing our adult children to live their own lives.

Forgiving Yourself

Letting go also means not blaming ourselves when our grown sons and daughters slip or fall: if they turn from the faith, their marriage fails, they do a poor job of rearing their children, or they commit another sin or make some other mistake. Dr. James Wilhoit, a professor of Christian education at Wheaton College, tells of hearing a couple say that they could finally relax as parents when their grandchildren had married Christians. He adds: *How sad. As Christian parents we must do all we can to rear our children according to biblical principles, with love and discipline. But then we have to trust God for the outcome. If our adult children mess up their lives, it's not our fault. They are responsible for their own sins and mistakes. At some point we have to say, "We've done all we can before God. Our children are in his hands."*

Letting go means understanding that your children are grown and are responsible for their own lives. You continue to love your sons and daughters, to pray, and to offer counsel and help, but you are not responsible for what they make of life. If they mess up, it's not your fault.

In order to grow up and to make a marriage work, young men and women must leave home. We must let our children go.

2. Offer Your Blessing

Regardless of the relationship or age, your children need your blessing—to be told that they are valued, that you believe in them, and that they are headed in the right direction. Your sons and daughters needed your blessing after high school, and they need it now, before the wedding.

This comes easily when your child has done well and when you are convinced the spouse-to-be is just perfect for your child. But still you need to say it . . . or write it. Better yet, do both—write your feelings, expressing your pride at what you have seen in your child as they have matured, your pleasure in their lifestyle and decisions (including the choice of a mate), and your pledge to pray for and encourage them in the future. Be specific, tracing God's work in your child's life from birth till this moment. End by saying specifically: *I now give you my blessing, trusting you fully to God with the confidence that "he who began a good work in you will carry it on to completion until the day of Christ Jesus" (Philippians 1:6, NIV).*

Make this a special occasion. Take your child to breakfast or lunch or to a favorite spot, read them what you have written, give it to them, and pray together. Some parents give their child a small gift or a Bible as a remembrance of this moment.

That's the ideal. But what should you do if you believe that your child is making a terrible mistake in the choice of a husband or wife? First, you should lovingly share your concerns. Describe your feelings and state your case, being careful to explain your reasons. If you have a good relationship with your child, they still may react negatively or defensively at first, but eventually will probably be open to your counsel.

Jennifer Luttrell had graduated from college and was living and working about a thousand miles from her parents. During the summer, however, she met a guy and fell hard. She was even talking about getting married after knowing him for just a short time. In fact, her plan was to quit her job, sell her car, and move close to this young man as soon as she could. Lew and Dottye explain: *We didn't feel good at all about the relationship and how quickly it had developed. We shared our concerns with Jennifer in a long letter. She didn't take it well. But she remembered "Honor your father and mother" and was serious about her Christian commitment, so she took the letter to her pastor. He advised her to take our counsel seriously and to slow down. Eventually she ended the relationship. Looking back, Jen can't see why she ever was infatuated with that young man. We thank God for his work in her life.*

If your child rejects your advice and is determined to push ahead with the wedding, *resist the temptation to vent your anger and frustration.* It won't be easy, but look for a way to affirm your child without giving approval to what they are doing. This doesn't mean that you should present your child with a blank check and go along with whatever they want. You should not compromise your basic beliefs, but you should affirm the person and your love even while expressing your displeasure and disapproval of their plans. Consider again the parable of the Prodigal Son. The son knew of his father's love, and the father stood waiting and watching, ready to forgive his lost son.

Your children need to be assured of your love, regardless of their age or situation in life.

3. Build the Friendship

Parents have an excellent opportunity to relate as peers and friends and not just as mothers and fathers to their adult children. Over the years I have appreciated the strong friendship that Gail and her mother enjoy. May Bright will always be Gail Veerman's mother and will be honored by Gail as such, but they relate on level ground. I felt as though I had a similar relationship with my parents, especially with my father during his last few years when he was struggling to care for Mom. We met once a week for lunch (each of us would drive forty-five minutes) and talked—as father and son but also as friends.

Friendships need time and communication in order to flourish and grow strong. Waving good-bye at the church after the wedding shouldn't mean shutting yourself out of your child's life. Getting married signals a loss of control, not a loss of influence. Hopefully, your children will want to tell you about what is going on in their lives and will still come to you for advice. But don't wait for them to make the first move. Give the newlyweds a call, drop them a line, or, if they're in the area, take them out for dinner.

When you're thinking about spending the rest of your lives together, you're usually so head over heels in love that you ignore weaknesses, foibles, differences, and idiosyncrasies. Those may become major irritations in the months and years to come, but they're nothing that should jeopardize the future of the marriage. Too often, people not committed to the sanctity and permanence of marriage find themselves letting the "D" word into their conversation and arguments. Before you know it, they're seriously considering splitting.

Jerry B. Jenkins, As You Leave Home (Colorado Springs: Focus on the Family, 1993), p. 125.

Treat your adult sons and daughters as adults. Don't talk down to them or dispense unsolicited advice as you would to a small child. Instead, listen carefully to what they say, demonstrate respect for their opinions, and ask for advice and help.

Also, work at building a relationship with the other half of the couple—your son-in-law or daughter-in-law. I have always appreciated the way Gail's parents have treated me: as a son, as an adult, and as a member of the family. I hope I do the same someday with my sons-in-law.

Look for ways to build a solid friendship with your adult child and their new spouse.

A child's wedding can be stressful for parents, no matter where the child falls in the birth order. In addition to the complications and cost of the ceremony, the wedding marks a new stage in the child's life—the beginning of life together and a new family arrangement. In order to allow your children to become fully independent individuals and to begin to relate to them as adults, you need to *let go, offer your blessing,* and *build a new kind of friendship.*

LET'S THINK ABOUT IT

Warnings

- *Don't hold on to your adult sons and daughters.* Let them go and grow.
- *Don't try to plan the wedding.* The wedding belongs to the couple.
- *Don't drive your child away with sarcasm or judgments.* Even when your adult child is wrong, respond with love. You can reject the action and still accept the person.
- *Don't continue to treat your adult child as a little child.* You will always be the parent, but now you are both adults and, thus, peers.

Opportunities

- *As you plan the wedding together, talk to your child about marriage* and offer books to read, tapes to listen to, and other helpful resources.
- *Express your love for your child by giving your blessing.* This passage is a big event for both of you (see Genesis 27:31-34).
- *Use the wedding and the time preparing for it as a bridge to a strong friendship with your child.* Communicate that you value your adult child as a person and are open to their advice.

- *Allow the trauma of this event to build your faith* (see James 1:2-7).
- *Treat your daughter-in-law or son-in-law as a valued member of the family.*

Lessons

- *Our children grow so quickly.* It seems as though they just got here and suddenly they are gone. We must make the most of our time with them.
- *Weddings can be very emotional occasions.* But through our tears, we can celebrate our children's maturity, commitment to Christ, and plans for the future.
- *Life is constantly changing.* We must find our security in God and his Word.

Resources

- Howard Hendricks, Jeanne Hendricks, and LaVonne Neff, eds., *Husbands and Wives* (Wheaton, Ill.: Victor, 1988). In this outstanding resource, the editors have compiled hundreds of articles from dozens of experts, covering every imaginable topic related to marriage.
- Ruth Muzzy and R. Kent Hughes, *The Christian Wedding Planner* (Wheaton, Ill.: Tyndale House, 1991). This book is spiral-bound for easy use. Filled with forms, checklists, and timelines, it has everything the bride and groom need to know from engagement to honeymoon in planning their wedding celebration.

Emptying
the House

━━━━━〜━━━━━

10

The canoe weighed heavily on the shoulders of the two explorers as they continued their determined walk down the path through the dense forest to the river. Although others had taken this route and had returned with captivating tales, this was *their* first attempt on this challenging ribbon of water. With each step their excitement grew at the adventure ahead. Finally they arrived at the clearing. Placing the canoe on the muddy banks, they prepared themselves for the journey, tying their supplies securely and donning life jackets and helmets. After easing the canoe into the water and kneeling in the bow and stern, they pushed off and moved quickly to the center of the stream. At first the current was slow, so they pulled on the paddles to guide and propel them forward. But shortly they were moving swiftly, carried by the river, and only needed the paddles for steering.

Drawn by the current, they eased around turns and under branches. Surrounded by the silent forest and the steady gurgling of the stream, they marveled at the beauty and laughed when they surprised a deer around one bend of the river, sending him crashing back through the underbrush. The trip was all they had imagined.

A few turns later, they became aware of a low, roaring sound in the distance. As the sound grew louder, the pace and intensity of the river seemed to increase. Soon they were hurtling forward, exhilarated by the speed but a little anxious about the source of the roar.

Suddenly they were caught in the grip of the current, and they plunged ahead. The sound of crashing water grew deafening as the river began to drop and cascade over and around rocks. Straining against the paddles, they fought to keep the canoe pointed forward. A huge boulder loomed before them and blocked their way, but just before the imminent collision, they turned the bow and veered around it. But then the trunk of a fallen tree threatened to tip the canoe and pour the two into the swirling stream. With a screech of aluminum on bark, they forced the canoe to the right and avoided disaster. Then to the right again . . . and left . . . and right . . . and down—scraping and leaving silver streaks on rocks at both sides. As the water churned and threatened to capsize their boat, they continued the feverish pace down the river—soaked to the skin, knees bleeding, and muscles aching. The thrill of the adventure had long been replaced by pain, fear, and longing for relief. Perhaps they had passed deer, eagles, beavers, otters, owls, lush fauna, and fascinating flora, but consumed by keeping their craft afloat and even surviving, they had not noticed.

The river seemed to wind forever, relentlessly and recklessly pulling the canoe with its rushing current and swirling eddies, fighting against the explorers as if to expel them as unwanted intruders. Then with a sudden twist to the left, they hurtled downward at a dangerous angle as the river dropped beneath them. Gasping for breath, they could only hold the sides of the canoe, struggle to keep their balance, and pray that they wouldn't capsize or smash against the rocks below.

Suddenly they burst free of the chaos. With the roar retreating quickly behind them, they were surrounded by quiet as the river spilled them into a lake. Battered, bruised, and bent from exhaustion, they coasted forward, relieved to be safe but almost too tired to care.

Parents navigate a similar route. Thrilled by the prospect of a new baby, they begin the journey. It seems peaceful enough, but soon they encounter turbulence as life's current pulls them first one way and then another. Around boulders of marriage adjustments, childhood growing pains, and financial stress, they rush toward the teenage rapids with its own emotional white-water ride. Through junior high, senior high, and beyond, the pace seems to quicken and the threatening obstacles increase. Then suddenly the kids are gone, and Mom and Dad are alone in the calm.

While this peaceful lake would seem to be a welcome relief after the previous nine passages of parenting, it presents its own set of emotions and challenges. In fact, some parents find this to be the most difficult passage of all. I find three common reactions by parents during this time of life.

CAPSIZING

Strange as it may seem, just when the marriage vessel has weathered all the storms and has endured all the trials of child rearing, it tips, in what should be calm waters. In reality, the traveling companions capsize their own canoe.

Some troubled marriages stay together well beyond the crisis point "for the sake of the children." Rather than resolve their differences and work to improve their relationship and rekindle the flame of love, these men and women simply endure each other until the children are gone.

In some cases the husband or wife goes through midlife crisis. As the youngest child prepares to leave home, they sense that life is slipping away and try to recapture youth. Sometimes this takes the form of a sexual affair with a younger woman or man, causing irreparable damage to the marriage.

For other couples, their whole life together has centered

around the children: driving them places, solving their problems, and meeting their needs. Perhaps the first baby came nine months after the wedding (or sooner), so the husband and wife had virtually no time to spend together, just the two of them, getting to know each other and building a solid foundation for their relationship. For eighteen years or more, they have busily attended to their children. When the last child leaves and they are left alone, they suddenly realize that they do not know each other—or worse yet, that they don't like each other.

In all three situations, the marriage dissolves when the nest is empty. The director of counseling at a Christian college told me that he hears about a staggering number of divorce proceedings in September and October. As soon as the students, usually the youngest children in these families, left for college, the marriages fell apart.

RECOVERING

Many couples stay together but struggle with the prospect of having just the two of them at home. Like exhausted canoeists coasting into the lake, they are consumed with conflicting feelings and may even find the peaceful calm a bit disconcerting.

An "empty nest" presents new challenges in any marriage. But it need not mean "midlife crisis." In a relationship built on love, respect, and commitment, there are mutual goals, though each partner may prefer a different route or speed level. If you remember that you are both heading in the same general direction, it will be easier to merge traffic, even if one or the other needs to yield the right-of-way temporarily.

Open communication—correctly interpreting the words and actions of a loved one—eases the traffic flow and forestalls dangerous collisions. By keeping open the lines of verbal give-and-take, we can reach new understanding and a satisfactory resolution of conflict.

Dennis Gibson and Ruth Gibson, The Sandwich Years (Grand Rapids: Baker, 1991), p. 158.

Loneliness

Even in solid marriages, parents admit to feeling empty and alone when all the children have left. We have strong hints of this experience during other passages, especially when we send our older kids, one at a time, off to college, the military, work, or marriage. These feelings are intensified when the last child leaves.

Gail and I felt our loss deeply when Kara left for college, but then most of our attention shifted to Dana. Of course, we still keep in touch with Kara, seeing her during vacation breaks, writing letters, and talking on the phone. But day to day we focus on Dana and her high school activities. Even with Kara gone, our lives are filled with athletic practices and games, music rehearsals and performances, youth group activities, and discussions of homework, friends, expectations, plans, schedules, and rules. I can't imagine what it will be like around here in a few years, especially at dinner, with both of them gone.

When I asked Anne Davis what she and her husband, Dick, missed most, she answered: *I miss the laughter, the phone calls, and the excitement. I don't miss the "Oh, Mom!" stuff. But I miss the upbeatness of both the kids. Now it's very quiet.*

Especially at first, the empty nest can be lonely.

Awkwardness

Because many couples' lives have revolved totally around their children, the kids' departure leaves these parents feeling awkward with each other and themselves. Larry Kreider explains: *At first you sit in the silence and think, "What did we talk about before we had kids?" You also begin to realize why couples get divorced after the children leave home—they hadn't spent time during those years filling each other's emotional tanks, and now they are empty.*

Husbands and wives can feel awkward as they try to fill the silence and relate to each other again. Larry adds: *It's like starting over. You ask, "Where can we go? What can we do?" It has all been put on hold for eighteen to twenty years.*

Stress

Marriages are subjected to great stress as soon as all the kids leave home. A common source of stress is financial. My parents put five children through private Christian colleges. They had sixteen or seventeen consecutive years of college payments and eventually invested a tremendous amount of money in our higher education. By the time a couple gets to the last child, their finances may be stretched to the limit.

Another source of stress can be the problems of the grown children. If a child struggles or fails (in school, in marriage, or in a job), each spouse can blame the other for the problems, accusing with "I told you so" barbs.

Relief

Some couples feel relieved during this passage, as though a great burden has been lifted from their backs. Maybe a child has found it difficult to become independent and leave home. Perhaps a grown child had returned for one reason or another. For these parents, having the home empty is a positive sign of progress in their kids' lives.

As a couple moves from the middle years—with all the busyness of piano lessons, practice sessions, recitals, and involvment in Child Evangelism clubs, Youth for Christ, vacation Bible school, etc.—and the children leave the nest, you find yourself immersed in the needs of aging parents and a new set of demands. For us, becoming grandparents was a bright, sparkling experience. And the sparkle hasn't tarnished.

Joan and Bob Biastock

Chuck Lewis says: *Sue and I felt considerable relief. Our youngest lived at home and went to a local junior college for a couple of years after graduation. Although Dan had more freedom, it was still a lot like when he was in high school. Sue, especially, had trouble resting until he came home at night.*

When Dan went off to New York to finish college, we felt freed from a sense of obligation and responsibility. Now we can recapture our time together without filtering it through our children's schedules.

Karen and Neal Voke's youngest child, Jason, had tried college three times, but he was floundering in terms of his future. Karen explains: *Jason lived at home with us through most of the college thing. But when he went to the city to study film and video, he was ready to get out. And we were ready, too. Neal and I thought it would be a wise investment for all of us if we could find an apartment that he could share with someone else or that we could afford, and count that as room and board that we would have been paying at college. So Jason has been in his own apartment for a couple of years now. He enjoys his studies, and he is looking better and feeling better about him-self—finally.*

It can be a relief to know that, for better or worse, our job as parents is nearly finished and that our children can make it on their own.

Adjustment

Another part of the recovery process is adjusting to our changing roles. We may have been doing this for several years now, but it peaks during this passage. The change is from a relationship where we, as parents, are always in control and meeting our children's needs to a peer relationship where we and our children talk as adults and meet each other's needs.

Making this adjustment can be especially difficult for some women who have spent most of their adult lives being mothers. They have taken care of their sons and daughters and have gained much of their self-worth from their children. It's not easy to back off and be their child's friend. Jim Green says: *Usually, it is the mom who is in the nesting business. When her children are gone, it can be disastrous. She then may start to "mother" her husband. I see this all the time in my ministry. Judy and I were able to avoid this in our marriage because we talked about it ahead of time and she was able to channel her interests and mothering instincts in another direction. Then, when grandchildren came along, she found it very fulfilling to help Jana with the kids. Sometimes this need to "mother" makes women push their married daughters to have children.*

I remember going through a similar era in my own life. My parents handled me wisely in those years, and it was rare to have them stumble into common parental mistakes. However, we had been a very close-knit family, and it was difficult for my mother to shift gears when I graduated from high school. During that summer, I traveled 1,500 miles from home and entered a college in California. I will never forget the exhilarating feeling of freedom that swept over me that fall. It was not that I wanted to do anything evil or previously forbidden. It was simply that I felt accountable for my own life and did not have to explain my actions to my parents. It was like a fresh, cool breeze on a spring morning. Young adults who have not been properly trained for that moment sometimes go berserk in the absence of authority, but I did not. I did, however, quickly become addicted to that freedom and was not inclined to give it up.

Dr. James Dobson, Parenting Isn't for Cowards (Dallas: Word, 1987), pp. 211–212.

Larry Kreider adds: *Having both kids gone was a big adjustment for Susan—she still needed an expression of her desire to serve and meet needs. Susan found an outlet at church, where she became very involved.*

Anne Davis relates that it wasn't too difficult for her and Dick when their daughter Carrie left for college because their son had already gone and Carrie was attending college closer to home. Then she adds: *When Carrie transferred to a college in Atlanta the next year, it was a little tougher on us. But I knew she wasn't really leaving yet. In fact, she called all the time to tell me about what's going on in her life. But the day was coming.* For Anne and Dick, the nest is emptying gradually.

Another kind of adjustment is described by Dottye

Luttrell: *It's hard for some women to see their once young and gangly daughters outshine them. Mom still wants that female dominance. But after you get through that, it's really nice having a comfortable friendship, where advice is looked for and appreciated.* Men may also have difficulty seeing their sons pass them up: achieving more, earning more, leading more, or gaining more notoriety.

These adjustments can be awkward and even painful, but they are important to make if we are going to recover from the harrowing parenting journey and move through this passage.

PADDLING ON

Returning to the canoeing analogy, consider the couple who have successfully navigated the parenting river and have recovered from the ordeal and the change from chaos to calm. At this point they begin a new journey together and are free to enjoy the scenery and each other's company. Parents can discover many advantages to being *home alone.*

Time

The benefit discovered first by most couples is the increase in discretionary time. Parents don't realize how much they invest each day in their children and how much their lives revolve around their children's activities and needs. Kids also take time to feed, clothe, clean, counsel, and pick up after. Susan Kreider says, "We don't have the messy rooms anymore, so now it takes half the time to clean the house."

Children leave a gigantic hole in the schedule when they leave.

We can use this time constructively. Larry Kreider adds, "Susan and I now have time to talk and do things together. I discovered that I have time to reflect, relax, read, study, and get more involved in church."

When the kids leave, we gain precious time.

Freedom

While children are gaining their freedom from their parents, Mom and Dad are gaining freedom from their kids. Children undeniably tie a couple down. We discovered that truth in the second passage of parenting. Many couples are shocked to realize that they can't drop everything, as they did before the baby was born, and run to the church for a meeting, across town to a social event, or even next door for a cup of coffee. The child is always a concern. The comedian Gallagher uses a bowling ball with a diaper on it, attached to his leg, to symbolize a new baby and parent. The new family member is attached, can be a heavy burden to bear, and can make mobility very difficult.

Even older children take enormous time, energy, and money. When Dana was in junior high, I coached soccer, basketball, and softball, timed at swim meets, helped at school, and attended all her events. Now that she is in high school, my coaching days are over, but I still drive her everywhere, help with choir parents, serve on the principal's parent council, and go to all her games and performances. Even though Gail and I will still try to be involved in Dana's life after high school, it won't be the same. We will be free to invest ourselves elsewhere.

Many couples take advantage of this freedom and invest their time in each other. Jim Green says, "Judy and I started dating more. Often we will just take off and go somewhere together."

One woman shared that another benefit of this new freedom is that she and her husband can make love with the bedroom door open. They don't have to worry anymore about being interrupted.

Anne Davis says: *Dick and I have been able to get to know each other better. We go out to dinner more than we used to when the kids were home, and we have date nights. There is much more spontaneity in our marriage. And I appreciate the closeness. We've grown together—it's a very comfortable feeling.*

Rachel Ringenberg recalls that she and Gerald were excited when their youngest child, Jeff, left for college. "We were going to have fun. We would be able to travel, play golf, and go to Jeff's basketball games."

We can put our new freedom to good use.

Quiet

The most frequently used adjective to describe what it's like to have the kids gone is *quiet*. Teenagers' lives seem to be brimming with exciting activities. Phones ring or friends drop by; discussions arise over dating, using the car, or extending the curfew; arguments rise and fall; TV sets glare and stereos blare. With boundless energy, adolescents live in continuous motion and carry their parents with them. Even the days leading to their exit swirl with a whirlwind of activity, including shopping, packing, and good-byes to friends. Then Mom and Dad return home from the university, wedding, apartment, or airport, and silence engulfs them.

Although this dramatic change can be interpreted negatively as loneliness and loss, it also can be very positive. We can take advantage of this quiet to spend time in the Word and in prayer: "Be still, and know that I am God" (Psalm 46:10, NIV). We can read, think, journal, and plan. We can reduce the stress in our lives.

Larry Kreider says: *It became very peaceful in the house. When the kids came back home and we had to readjust to the noise and activity, I realized that I was no longer living in that former pattern.*

Although it may take time to adjust to a home without children, we can discover and take advantage of the time, freedom, and quiet that this parenting passage provides.

HOW TO RESPOND

1. Relate to Each Other

Just two people live in the house now—Mom and Dad, facing each other across the dinner table, with no other people to deflect attention and take time, and no other relationships to build or maintain. If the couple has a poor relationship, this stress can fracture the marriage as husband and wife shudder at the prospect of spending the rest of their lives together. But even in good marriages, where the relationship has been nurtured over the years and where divorce is not considered to be an option, husbands and wives will feel the stress and will have to adjust to this dramatic change in their lives.

It will be a challenge, but you can use the time, freedom, and quiet to reduce the stress, to improve your relationship with your spouse, and to build your marriage. You can relate to each other again as spouse, friend, and lover—rather than coparent.

Be Intentional

Don't make the mistake of thinking you can sit back, relax, and let your mate do all the changing and work. Instead, seize the initiative and actively seek to improve your relationship. Perhaps the easiest way to begin is to find an activity that you can do together.

One husband told me that his wife does all the shopping. He doesn't enjoy shopping and has always resisted trips to the mall or grocery store. Shopping would be a great way for this couple to spend time together when the kids have gone, but the husband will have to take the initiative.

A wife shared that her husband enjoys attending athletic events, but she has never cared much about sports unless their kids were playing in the games. This woman could spend time with her husband by suggesting that they go to a game together.

Another woman decided to take up jogging. Her husband runs three miles several times a week and would enjoy the company.

At first, these kinds of shared activities may not be fun for you, but they will give you the opportunity to spend time with your husband or wife and will provide grist for conversation.

Another possibility is to find a *new* activity to do together. You could both take a class in tennis or golf and then participate in that sport regularly. You could join a health club and work out together a few times a week. You could choose a mystery series or collection of great books, then read and discuss them. You could volunteer your time at church, a nursing home, or a charity. You could redecorate the house, work in the garden, build a bookcase, take up square dancing, join a bowling team, refinish furniture, lead a church-growth group, or write a novel. You shouldn't have too much difficulty finding something to do together.

The important point is that *you* take the initiative and make a determined effort to improve your friendship with your spouse.

Be Creative

Remember when you began to date the man or woman who is now your spouse? You worked hard at being romantic—making a good impression and expressing your feelings in just the right way. Flowers, cards, candlelight dinners, snow angels, walks in the park, mystery dates, little gifts, and fancy restaurants were all part of your repertoire. You probably have a great story about how you gave or received the engagement ring. But over the years, you both have settled into a comfortable rut. After all, you said your vows and settled the matter—you don't have to impress anyone anymore.

In addition, for the past two or three decades, most of

your available minutes, dollars, and energy have been directed toward the kids. You may not have had much time for romance or money for dates.

But now you're back to just the two of you, and you need to rekindle the relationship—to get to know each other more fully. Most of your excuses for not doing anything together, just the two of you, left with the kids. So use your imagination and be creative. Think of what you could do together that would be enjoyable, perhaps even romantic, and would lead to talk and intimacy. You could plan a mystery date, complete with coded clues. On a cold night, you could rent a video, make a favorite snack, build a fire in the fireplace, and then snuggle, eat, and watch the movie together. You could write short love notes and leave them in your mate's pockets, wallet, or car. You could surprise your spouse with tickets to a Broadway production, a play, or their favorite soloist or music group.

There is almost no limit to what you can do to have fun together. Be creative—go for it!

Be Spontaneous

Before your first child was born, you were free to visit friends in another city for the weekend, go out for lunch after church, go out to dinner any night of the week, or make a surprise visit to your folks. With children came restraints on your time and money. You had to plan ahead, clear every new event with the family calendar, and line up baby-sitters. And you had to guard your checkbook because of the additional mouths to feed. Now those restraints have been loosened. You can alter your plans on a whim and change directions in a flash.

Of course, that's easier to write or say than to do. After twenty-plus years of living one way—conservatively watching your time and money and trying hard to be a responsible parent—it may feel awkward, or even impossible, to live with seemingly reckless abandon. But adding a touch of spontaneity can work wonders in your relationship.

Go to a unique, ethnic restaurant; surprise your spouse at work and take them to lunch; go to a spa together and get the full treatment; plan an escape weekend; drive to a nearby town that you've never visited; have a picnic; go on a summer missions project; accompany your husband or wife on a business trip. In short, rediscover each other.

To build your relationship, be intentional, be creative, and be spontaneous. In whatever you do together, remember to talk, listen, and affirm your spouse in love (see 1 Corinthians 13).

2. Relate to Your Children

Our children are now independent and (hopefully) mature. But even as adults, they are still our chiildren, and we are still their parents. So how, then, do we build a friend and peer relationship with our grown sons and daughters?

Back Off

The first step is to retreat a bit and give your child some space. Jim and Judy Green's kids still live in the area. Jim says: *It's good having them close, but we can't treat them as children. They need our affection, but not condescension, interference, or unasked-for advice.*

This can be tough for parents who are accustomed to having the last word and always being right. They still want to tell their kids how to spend their money, where to live, when to have children, how to vote, and where to go to church. Others just find it difficult to relate in anything other than the role of parent. Or they just don't want to admit that their kids have grown up.

Art Wittmann confesses that, during an especially difficult time with one of his teenage daughters, he said, "I'll be so glad when they're grown up and on their own." Carol quickly told him not to talk that way because he would hate it when they were gone. Recently, after their daughter Kelly graduated from college, she returned to live at home for a couple of months. Art says: *One day she was talking about moving to an apartment with a girlfriend, and believe it or not, I tried to talk her out of it! This time Carol had to take me aside and tell me, "Let her go!"* Carol adds: *Kelly needed to get out. Everything was too easy at home.* Art concludes: *My relationship with all three girls has moved beyond the season of being a parent—it's a different type of relationship.*

Some parents have a codependent relationship with their children, in which they continue to play the roles of parent and child. A mother may think, *My daughter needs me!* and her daughter may think, *My mother needs me!* That's not a healthy relationship for anyone involved. The child needs to *leave home* completely, and the parent needs to deal with it and get on with life.

At this parenting passage, when all of your kids have left home, back off, especially from the youngest one, and give them space and time to establish their own lives as adults.

Stay Close

This next step may sound contradictory to the first, but *stay close.* Don't back off so far that you are out of your kids' lives completely. If your kids live many miles and hours away, check in by phone to see how they're doing or drop them a line. This is especially important the first few years after high school—they may find the separation as painful as you do. Your contact will assure them of your love and support.

Anne Davis says: *Dick has been really good about writing the kids letters. He's tender and his letters are heartfelt. He will write five pages at a time. Austin and Carrie have saved them all.*

Let your adult child know that you are rooting for them to make it in the adult world—you are their biggest fan. Ask specific questions about their life. When you express how much you miss them, also tell them about the new and exciting activities in which you and your spouse are involved. Let your child know that you are growing and changing, too.

We've had bad luck with our kids—they're all grown up.

Christopher Morley

Chuck Lewis shares that when their son Dan returned home during his school break, initially he and Sue had a good feeling about his being home. But then the worrying began again because he would come home long after they had gone to bed. Chuck says: *It was almost as though he was like an intruder in our lives. Dan and I had a heart-to-heart talk about the situation. I explained that we wanted to be sensitive to him but that we wanted him to reciprocate. He listened carefully and reacted very well. It's a delight to see him becoming an adult and taking responsibility for his actions.*

Keep in touch with your kids.

Open Up

Eventually you will have the opportunity to be vulnerable with your adult children, to open up and share your hurts, problems, and concerns. Again, this step is difficult for many parents because they find it much more comfortable to relate *down* to their kids instead of *across*. But opening up will enhance your relationship and build friendship.

My father was a very strong presence in our home. Because he was a firm disciplinarian, I didn't ever want him to be upset with me. He was also confident and decisive—he knew what he wanted to do and then did it. I grew up thinking Dad knew everything and didn't need much of anything. Perhaps the greatest compliment Dad ever paid me as an adult was to ask for my advice. He had been offered a position with a company in another city, and he asked my brothers, sister, and me what he should do. By sincerely asking for our input, Dad was treating us as adults.

Remember, too, that the older your children become, the more experience they have with life and the more they will be able to help you. Your kids can give wise counsel, helpful information, and heartfelt consolation.

Karen Voke shares: *After my mother died, Julie went down with me to take care of the funeral arrangements. She went back with me later, after we sold the house, to help me sort Mom's things. Julie put boxes together and passed everything by me. She wouldn't just make the decision. She knew that the little things meant as much to me as the big items, and I appreciated that. She and Jason have both been there for me in the last few years. They'll say, "It's OK, Mom, to feel the way you do." And I need to be told that. My kids played turnabout with me, and that's all right. It's good for children to see their parents hurting and to be there.*

Open up to your adult children. You will help them mature as independent adults, and you'll gain from their insight—they have much to give.

As you leave the river and enter into the peaceful pond, with no children at home, use your time, freedom, and quiet to rekindle the romantic flame *with your spouse* and to build an adult friendship *with your children*.

LET'S THINK ABOUT IT

Warnings

- *Having a suddenly empty and quiet house can be a shock.* You can feel lost and lonely.
- *Don't allow the stress of the empty nest to fracture your*

marriage. Stress can come from financial pressure, relationship strains, guilt, and children's problems.

- *Don't cling to your last child.* Let them go and become an adult.
- *Don't become consumed with worry about your kids who have left home.* Commit them to God and trust him to work in their lives.

Opportunities

- *Take advantage of your newfound time, freedom, and quiet.* Spend time with God and with your mate.
- *Take the initiative in building your relationship with your spouse.* Use your creativity and be spontaneous.
- *Allow your children to mature as adults.* Back off, giving them room to grow.
- *Allow your children to help you with your problems.* Open up to them, honestly sharing your concerns and dreams.

Lessons

- *Marriage is tested when the children leave home.* It's back to the couple, just two people in the house.
- *There's life after children,* and many opportunities for personal growth and enrichment.
- *Adults are responsible for their own mistakes*—even our children. It's not our fault when they fail or fall.
- *Grown children still need their parents, but as loving friends.*

♦ *When kids leave their parents, both need to adjust to the changing relationship.*

Resources

♦ Dave Arp and Claudia Arp, *52 Dates for You and Your Mate* (Nashville: Nelson, 1993). This is a great resource for creative dating ideas for married couples.

♦ Dave Veerman and Gail Veerman, *Getting Your Husband to Talk* (Wheaton, Ill.: Tyndale House, 1994). We've packed more than one hundred ideas into this little book to help wives start conversations with their husbands. If only one of the ideas works for you, it will be well worth the investment.

Beginning Again

11

A *Grandmother* Is . . .
. . . a big warm lap
. . . sweet smells in the kitchen
. . . chicken and dumplings and apple pie
. . . gifts and clothes sewn with care
. . . soft and tender hugs
. . . a card with money on every birthday

293

. . . congratulations, affirmations, exhortations

A Grandfather Is . . .
. . . candy in the shirt pocket
. . . a welcome, come-up-here, rocking-chair lap
. . . the distinctive smell of aftershave on mature skin
. . . tools in the garage and puttering in the basement
. . . stories about Mom or Dad as a child
. . . Thanksgiving prayers
. . . congratulations, affirmations, exhortations

I'm sure you could add scores of poignant feelings, smells, impressions, and memories. Do you remember the trips to your grandparents' house as a child? It may not have been "over the river and through the woods," but I imagine that your excitement built with each passing mile. There's something special about visiting Grandma and Grandpa!

Sooner than we may have expected, we are on the other side. Instead of packing up and driving (or flying) to Grandma and Grandpa's house, we are waiting for the visits, for the precious moments that we can spend with our children and our grandchildren. This parenting passage is very special and filled with emotions, opportunities, and challenges. Though last, many parents say it's the best.

THE FEELING FACTORS

As with all the passages, the emotions in this one are mixed, but most of them are positive. For better or worse, we have weathered the storms of parenting and have adjusted to having our children grown and gone. Now, life has come full circle, and we get to watch our children repeat the process. A number of factors will affect how we feel when our children have children.

Grandparents can be quite young (in their forties) or quite old. Younger grandparents probably will still be employed, healthy, and mobile. At the other extreme, Grandpa and Grandma will be retired and may have time and money, but they may not be in good health and may not be able to travel.

Years ago, extended families tended to stay close geographically. These days, however, siblings may be scattered across the world, hundreds—if not thousands—of miles away from Mom and Dad. When Kara was born, we lived in Illinois, an hour and a half from my parents. It was easy to get together with them for holidays, birthdays, or almost any time we wished. The situation changed drastically when we moved to Louisiana, where Dana was born. Then we could see my folks just once or perhaps twice a year. This was frustrating for us and for my parents.

Karen Voke explains that her daughter and husband, Lisa and Bob, moved to Germany with the military when their child (Karen and Neal's first grandchild) was two years old. While there, Lisa had another child. Karen explains: *They were our first grandchildren, and we felt cheated because they were so far away that we couldn't experience them. We also were jealous of our friends. We had played bridge with this one group for years—we were all about the same age. Everybody's kids were having kids, so these friends would parade in and tell about the weekend visits and all about their grandchildren. It was tough having Lisa and Bob so far away.*

The quality of our relationships with our kids will also affect how we feel when their children are born. Some parents enjoy good relationships with their adult children because they have been able to release and bless them. Because Gail and I enjoyed positive relationships with our parents, both sets of grandparents were thrilled at the birth of our daughters and wanted to be with them.

With many parents, however, the opposite is the case— they are frustrated, disappointed, or estranged from their children. They may even feel anger at the birth of a grandchild. In some situations, however, a grandchild can help reconcile adult children with their parents as the four adults now have parenting in common and the grandparents fall in love with the new baby.

The relationship with the daughter-in-law or son-in-law is another critical factor. We may be thrilled with our child's spouse and excited about their relationship and marriage. But that is not always the case. Parents may have been opposed to their child's choice of a mate. In another situation, the child's marriage may be struggling (or even abusive) and teetering on the edge of divorce. Or perhaps a bitter argument between parents and child or spouse has driven a wedge in the relationship. Some adults will even purposely hurt their parents by refusing to let them see their grandchildren. Obviously, all of these relational struggles can affect our feelings at this passage.

The timing of the grandchild is also a factor. Some

parents watch anxiously as their married sons and daughters struggle to conceive for many years. In some cases kids wait to get married, choose to remain childless for a number of years, and then finally have a child. At times, however, news of a pregnancy comes very soon, during a very difficult time in a marriage or against the advice of family and friends.

Sometimes, becoming a grandparent comes much sooner than you planned. Rhonda and Bob Childress explain that their oldest child, Andy, was a rebellious teenager in high school. A year after graduation, they insisted that he attend a Christian college where he had been offered a scholarship. Andy gave Bob and Rhonda a rough time during the first semester, but things changed when he met Janis. The next fall, motivated by love, he was much more eager to return to the college. Bob tells what happened next: *In late October or early November, Andy called and asked for both of us to be on the phone. I figured that he just wanted to discuss plans for Thanksgiving break. But then he said, "How do you feel about being grandparents?" Needless to say, we were shocked. Rhonda was so upset she couldn't talk. I was devastated, too, but we talked for about an hour and began to make plans for a December wedding.*

FEELINGS FROM
THE OTHER SIDE

These factors all combine to affect how we feel about a new grandchild, especially the first. Here are some of those feelings.

Joy and Love

The most prominent emotion at the birth of a grandchild is joy—the sheer delight in seeing a child become a parent and in welcoming a new member of the family into the world. Enfolding the baby in our arms elicits memories and emotions from when we held our tiny children so many years ago.

Understanding three simple keys to grandparenting infants will make this time a rewarding and joyful experience. The first key is to *be available.* New parents need help. . . . Parents need grandparents who are available to help with the multitude of chores during the baby's first year. Seemingly mundane tasks such as laundry, cooking, getting to the bank, and shopping can be difficult to accomplish as parents juggle schedules, work, and a young child.

The second key . . . is to *stay in the background.* Grandparents who want to be available also need to stay out of the way, in the background.

The third key . . . is simple yet probably the most important of all: *Enjoy the wonder.* Take time to be with your new grandchild; just hold her and thrill to the love this little life brings. Take time to enjoy the wonder of babies.

Jerry Schreur and Jack Schreur, Creative Grandparenting (Grand Rapids: Discovery House, 1992), p. 22.

Lorna Ray explains: *I was overwhelmed by the intensity of love that I felt, and the connectedness—Elizabeth would be part of me forever. I was excited that Bill and Sarah were having a baby, not that we were having a granddaughter. The baby pulled us closer, too. We have so much in common now.*

Sue and Chuck Lewis's daughter, Linda, lives in the Bahamas, far away from Mom and Dad. But Sue was able to fly there to be present when their first grandchild was born. It was a delightful mother-daughter experience.

Even when a child is born into less than ideal circumstances, we immediately love them—so innocent and vulnerable and part of the family. The child can pull us close to our children and their mates. Bob Childress explains: *After learning that Andy and Janis were expecting a baby, before marriage and before finishing college, one of my biggest frustrations for my son was that he wouldn't be able to experience more of life and build his relationship with Janis before becoming a father. But then I remembered Psalm 139 and the truth that God never made any of us by mistake. Even though the timing and the circumstances were difficult, this baby was created by God and was God's gift.*

The birth of a grandchild is a time for joy and celebration.

Responsibility

We also feel a sense of responsibility. As senior members of the family, we realize the necessity of being good examples, helpful counselors, and spiritual leaders.

Larry Kreider explains: *The title "grandparent" does something to me. It doesn't make me feel old, but it gives me a tremendous sense of spiritual responsibility. When I held Brett's son for the first time, I knew that I absolutely loved that child; yet I also realized that I was not ultimately responsible for his moral behavior. There's a certain relief and freedom that comes from that. But at the same time, I noticed as I held him that I almost wanted to be a patriarch. I wanted to put my hand on top of his head and bless him and pray for him. I do pray regularly for him, of course, but there's just this sense of spiritual connectedness. It was there, and strong, with my children, but it's even stronger with my grandson.*

Jay Kesler says:

> *Because the breakdown of societal values and the changes in society's mores are so subtle, grandparents can play an important role in stabilizing the lives of their grandchildren. They can become carriers of culture from one generation to the next, connecting links that keep society rooted in past values.*
>
> *Grandparents have the opportunity to pass on the experience-based wisdom that is missing in the lives of many young people today. And perhaps most important of all, grandparents can serve as spiritual catalysts to the younger generation, demonstrating for them the reality of life in Christ. (Grandparenting: The Agony & The Ecstasy. Ann Arbor, Mich.: Servant, 1993, pp. 13–14.)*

In their book, *Creative Grandparenting*, Jerry and Jack Schreur write:

Quite simply, grandparenting has become the most important part of our lives. It's bigger than our jobs, bigger than our plans for retirement, and much bigger than our dream of a relaxed life in a quiet house. We believe that being a grandparent is the best thing in the world. And after talking to hundreds of other grandparents, we've discovered that we are not alone. (Grand Rapids: Discovery House, 1992, p. 13.)

As grandparents, we have a great responsibility to pass along a spiritual heritage and our practical wisdom gained from years of living and rearing our own families.

Pride

The bumper sticker that reads "Ask me about my grandchildren" declares pride—Grandpa and Grandma are proud of their grandchildren and would love to tell us all about them.

No one likes braggarts—people who always talk about themselves and seem to think that everything they or their relatives do is absolutely the greatest. But there is nothing wrong with being proud of one's son, daughter, or grandchild. In fact, we should be our grandchildren's biggest fans. I remember my grandparents proudly introducing me to their friends and neighbors. And I remember how proud I was to be identified with them.

One of the biggest losses I felt after my dad and mom died was not being able to tell them about what Kara and Dana had accomplished recently. Gail's folks love hearing about the girls, and our family pictures adorn their apartment.

Grandparents feel justifiably proud of their grandchildren.

Loss

Regardless of the circumstances, grandparents can also feel a sense of loss. By doing simple addition, we can figure out that we may not be around to see this child as a teenager, college student, or adult. This is especially true with older grandparents. It's a fact of life that, eventually, every person dies. Grandchildren can remind us of our mortality.

Larry Kreider says: *Sometimes I feel as though time is running out for me. You never know what could happen, whether you're going to be around when this child grows to maturity. So I have that sense that time is passing and I ought to make every moment count.*

Mixed with the joy, love, responsibility, and pride can be sadness or loss—the feeling that we won't be around as long as we would like to enjoy these wonderful grandchildren.

Pain

Grandparenting can be painful when we are far from our children, when their marriages break up, or when their children are hurting. Bob Childress explains that, because of the strained relationship he and Rhonda had with their son, Andy, the news of the pregnancy brought them a lot of pain. But eventually, the baby helped bring healing to the relationship and enabled them to see evidence of spiritual maturity in Andy. Bob says: *Because of the distance and because Janis' parents were planning to be there when the baby was born, we planned to visit two weeks later. Andy called at 4:30 A.M. to announce that they were leaving for the hospital. His excitement was infectious. He called back two hours later with a different tone in his voice—the baby was experiencing stress and the doctors were discussing a C-section. Andy and Janis were afraid and wanted us to pray with them. We prayed, and the baby was delivered normally. Andy has three sisters who were pretty close to him, and by midafternoon, nothing could have kept us away from that hospital. Watching Andy experience the joy of holding his newborn son is something none of us will ever forget. I had the incredible privilege of holding that baby and praying, asking God's blessing on that new family and that new life with full knowledge that Andy and Janis agreed with my prayer and wanted God's hand on their family.*

In addition to joy, love, responsibility, pride, loss, and pain, we can feel anger, fear, disappointment, and hurt, depending on our relationships with our children and their spouses.

IMPORTANCE

Regardless of the mix of our emotions, the relationship between grandparents and grandchildren is important—to us, to our children, and to our grandchildren.

Importance to Us

Having grandchildren is important to us, first of all because they are our link to the future. Joe Coggeshall of the Christian Businessmen's Committee explains that too often we plan our lives as though everything ends when we die, at about eighty years of age. We fit our wedding, child rearing, career path, and retirement on this time line. In reality, he says, we ought to be thinking of about a 150-year span and working to influence at least three or four generations beyond our own. Having this perspective will influence how we live, spend our money, and invest our lives. Our grandchildren stand as the next step in that process.

In addition, grandchildren are important to us because they give us the chance to "do it better" the second time around. Many adults admit to being not-the-best parents. Often these men and women make wonderful grandparents as they shower their grandchildren with love and attention. Dennis and Ruth Gibson write:

> *When our friends in the sandwich years become grandparents, they tell us they get all the joys of having children without the headaches. This time around with infants, they say, they know what to expect better than they did as first-timers. (The Sandwich Years, Grand Rapids: Baker, 1991, p. 36.)*

We can put our parenting instincts and skills into action again.

Grandchildren are also important to grandparents because these wonderful boys and girls give *us* love, respect, and affection. In fact, kids often will listen to their grandparents even more than their parents. Bob Childress explains that before his grandson was born, he was playing golf with a friend and telling how he felt about becoming a grandfather. The friend began to say how "grandchildren are the greatest thing in the world," and Bob expected a familiar cliché to follow. But he was caught off guard when the friend said, "All children are born with rebellion in their heart, but it is rebellion against their parents, *not* their grandparents. They love their grandparents."

Joan Biastock says: *In the autumn of life, relationships change. Close friends move away, or their families and grand-children keep them busy and away from you. So you find a real need for warm, loving intimacy that grandchildren bring. One day, when Jimmy was about three years old, I met my daughter and the children at the mall. Jimmy was quiet and didn't seem excited to see me. However, as my daughter pushed the baby in the stroller, Jimmy walked with his hand in mine. After we had walked along for a while, I felt a strong tug on my arm. Jimmy was pulling on my hand. I knelt down because I wanted to look into his face, thinking that he wanted to tell me something. Jimmy never said a word; he just cupped my face in his hands and kissed me. That moment is captured in my heart to this day.*

I always looked forward to those visits to my grandparents' homes. I loved telling Grandma and Grandpa about school, sports, and music, and, later, about my love life. And I know how much those visits meant to them. Grandchildren can fill our lives with joy and excitement.

An added benefit is the joy the grandchild brings to other family members. Bob Childress says: *One of the most reward-ing experiences of this new grandchild is being able to watch Andy's younger sisters with their new nephew. This is the first experience they have had with a baby who was part of them.*

Because of the distance, they have only been with him for a short time, but there is a very strong bond.

Grandchildren are important to us.

Importance to Our Children

Though it is not always possible, every family should have at least one set of grandparents to affirm, love, advise, and connect to the past.

There are thousands of young people who need the advantage of surrogate grandparents in a much more desperate sense. Many children have never been around older people; they know nothing of the generations. . . . They desperately need contact with caring, Christian grandparents. I strongly urge mature Christians to look around the congregation and ask God to lay certain children on your heart. Search for those natural affinities and connections and begin the process of bringing these children under your wing.

Jay Kesler, Grandparenting: The Agony & the Ecstasy (Ann Arbor, Mich.: Servant, 1993), p. 162.

Grandparents can validate Mom and Dad's teachings, reinforcing the lessons with personal examples and putting present situations into a historical context. My grandparents survived the financial reversals and poverty of the Great Depression, but I had never known economic hardships. Without their perspective, I might have assumed that people had always lived the way I was living.

Grandparents are also important to parents because they can take up the slack in child rearing. For one reason or another, Mom and Dad won't be able to be at every activity, game, and performance of every child. If they live nearby, Grandma and Grandpa can attend many of these events, proudly videotaping, applauding, and cheering their grandchild.

Joan Biastock says: *As our grandchildren develop interests such as sports and school activities—all the things that increasingly occupy their time—we realize that we have been fortunate to have had the opportunities to spend so much quality time with them during these early formative years. We're thankful, too, that their parents have provided these opportunities by calling and inviting us to share in their children's lives.*

At times, Grandma and Grandpa can baby-sit, giving Mom and Dad a short break or vacation. But free child care shouldn't be abused, as Drs. Minirth, Newman, and Hemfelt explain:

> *Another trouble spot we find often is the interference in the couple's daily life posed by adult children and grandchildren. "If I had known grandchildren were so much fun, I would have had them first," says the grandmother. But if solid, comfortable boundaries are not in place, grandchildren and adult children can become too much of a good*

thing. The retired couple find themselves curtailing their own plans as they serve as hosts, baby-sitters, or emergency counselors. To an extent, this is good; older people have a wisdom and balance that youth need. Too much is not good. (Passages of Marriage, Nashville: Nelson, 1991, p. 276.)

Finally, grandparents are important to parents because they give them the opportunity to model God's command to "Honor your father and your mother" (Exodus 20:12, NIV). Children watch how Mom and Dad relate to *their* fathers and mothers, especially when they are old and in declining health. The chances are good that many years later the kids will repeat what they have seen with their own parents.

When my father was dying of congestive heart failure, my sister and brother-in-law, Barb and Charlie Havens, volunteered to let him stay with them under the care of a hospice. They gave him their bedroom, bringing in a hospital bed, oxygen, and other equipment. He lived in their home for six weeks until his death. Although it was a tremendous inconvenience for the Havens family, they honored Dad by caring for him. As I spent hours at his side, I thought about the great lesson my nieces, Jessica and Allison, were learning by their parents' godly example.

Importance to Our Grandchildren

Just as grandchildren provide hope for the future, Grandma and Grandpa provide an important link to the past, telling stories, providing family history, keeping family traditions alive, and making a cross-generational connection. Once, when Gail's father was in the hospital, we visited him as a family. Dad kept the girls entertained with stories of how he met their grandmother and how they lived when Gail was a little girl. Children need to interact with older people in order to broaden their perspective. In fact, if Grandma and Grandpa are no longer around, parents would be wise to find another older couple or two to act as surrogate grandparents.

Grandparents also play an important role as listeners. Children need someone with whom to talk, pour out their feelings, admit their fears, and share their dreams. Their friends don't understand or may not care, and Mom and Dad may get upset or want to argue. Grandma and Grandpa often provide a nonjudgmental sounding board.

Grandparents are also important because they will affirm their grandchildren's abilities, talents, and positive personality traits. Children need people to praise their art, music, grades, and athletic achievements. Although grandparents are admittedly prejudiced, their affirmation helps build confidence and self-esteem.

Finally, grandparents are important to grandchildren because they provide insight and wisdom gained through training and many years of experience. A few decades ago, I was amazed as I watched Gail's dad help me renovate our bathroom. He knew exactly what he was doing because he had renovated several houses during his lifetime. And when Kara and Dana were young, he loved to walk with them across his backyard to his garden, explain how to grow the biggest and best tomatoes, and let them help water and weed.

When Kara was in fifth grade, she had to choose a science project for school. I suggested that she report on ion exchange because Grandpa Veerman was an expert in that field. Dad enjoyed helping Kara with her display and experiment, and Kara ended up with an excellent project.

Grandma and Grandpa have much to offer children as links to the past, listeners, and sources of affirmation and wisdom.

RESOURCES

Clearly the grandparenting experience is important for us, our children, and our grandchildren. But at times we may feel as though time has passed us by and we have very little to offer. After all, technology is advancing at an alarming rate. Most of us have difficulty programming a VCR, and every day new, amazing products are introduced: cellular phones, CD-ROM, hand-held computers, window-ledge satellite dishes, the electronic highway, fiber optics, and on and on. Our grandchildren seem to know everything about these gadgets, while we barely know they exist.

In addition, children today are struggling with issues and problems that were virtually unheard of just a few years ago: AIDS, drugs, school violence, condoms, gangsta' rap, etc. We can easily feel out of touch and even in the way.

But we have much to offer. Consider these resources.

1. Expertise

No matter how pervasive the new technology, people still need to know skills that we have mastered: everything from how to handle money and how to study the Bible to how to make a cherry pie and how to fix a bicycle. With all of the emphasis on new appliances and machines, many have forgotten (or haven't learned) how to work with the old ones. But over the years, we have learned much about decorating, automobiles, writing, speaking, cooking, plumbing, planting, cleaning . . . the list is almost endless. We know plenty and have a lot to give.

2. Experience

We also have a wealth of experience. We have heard the rhetoric of dozens of political campaigns, cared for a broad array of physical maladies, traveled extensively, read count-less books, heard hundreds of sermons, held a number of jobs, fallen in love, taught classes and Bible studies, watched births and deaths, invested money, been hurt and have recovered, counseled friends and strangers, and thought through profound issues. Solomon exclaimed, "There is nothing new under the sun" (Ecclesiastes 1:9, NIV), so when a problem arises, we've seen it before and can tell how to solve it from our experience. We have knowledge and wis-dom that only experience can give.

3. Time

Although we may feel as though our years, months, and days are slipping away, we still have time to give. With the kids grown and gone, our schedules have become simplified. We're not too busy these days to take time to invest our lives in what is truly important. We have time to spend a week or two with a daughter when she comes home from the hospital with a new baby. We have time to take a boy or girl camping and fishing. We have time to make or shop for the perfect gift. We have time to watch and listen to our grandchildren. We have time to write letters . . . and to talk on the phone . . . and to hug. These days, time is a precious commodity, and we have it to give to our grandchildren.

Be wary of giving too many material gifts. (Especially do not create an arena of competition with the other grandparents.) Specialize in giving gifts of time and self: a walk, playing in the snow, making cookies, going fishing, reading a book, telling stories, talking together to Jesus.

Dennis Gibson and Ruth Gibson, The Sandwich Years (Grand Rapids: Baker, 1991), p. 37.

---

4. Money

I know that not every grandparent is financially independent. In fact, many struggle to live on their fixed income from Social Security or a company pension plan. But with the elimination of expenses such as college tuition, weddings, mortgage, etc., many grandparents are doing well financially. This is especially true for those who are in good health and are still working or those who have been able to invest well for their retirement. These men and women can use some of their money to travel to see the grandkids or to bring the kids to where they live. I know of grandparents who have given money for their grandchildren's college education and others who have underwritten the cost of a wonderful family vacation. We shouldn't throw money at our children and grandchildren, but we can use our financial resources to invest in the family and in the future.

Grandparents have much to offer their children and grandchildren.

HOW TO RESPOND

Given the importance of grandparenting and the resources we possess, here's how you can respond during this parenting passage.

1. Don't Interfere

When you see your child and their spouse making what seems to be a mistake in their parenting efforts, you will be tempted to jump in with a truckload of advice. Resist that temptation. Instead, let them rear their children *their* way and give them support in their parenting efforts. Jay Kesler says:

> *We've had our shot at parenting. We've done the best we could, and our children are the product of our work. Even our failures provide experience that makes us wiser, more*

patient, and more forgiving. Now, as grandparents, we become a support to our children as they attempt the confusing and demanding task of parenting.

I believe one of the major roles of the grandparent is to be cheerleader—that is, to encourage our children in their own parenting. We have already given advice in the form of our own theory of parenting and our own conduct over their entire lifetimes. Now is the time for encouragement and support. (Grandparenting: The Agony & The Ecstasy, Ann Arbor, Mich.: Servant, 1993, pp. 30–31.)

I have heard grandparents openly criticize their adult children for their handling of everything from childhood sickness to adolescent rebellion. Others have actually interfered directly in various parent-child situations. Not only is that foolish, it is wrong.

Your child doesn't need that kind of "help." Instead, be available and ready to offer suggestions when asked. Even then, carefully phrase your advice, framing it with love. For example, don't tear down the child: "Bradley is so selfish!" or "Julie seems to be lazy." Such harsh statements will only cause your child to become defensive. Parents can say anything they want about their own child, but if someone else says the same thing, the parents will feel attacked and personally insulted. You have much to share from your experience as a parent, even from your mistakes, but wait for the right time.

Just a few years ago (although it seems much longer) you were struggling with the other parenting passages. Undoubtedly, you knew that you were feeling your way through the process, doing your best, but not sure how to respond to every new parenting challenge. Even though you were painfully aware of your need, you would have resented condescending Here's-what-you-ought-to-do advice, even from someone you love. But you would have welcomed empathy, understanding, and Is-there-anything-I-can-do? availability. Use that as a guide for helping your kids as they move through each passage. They have to rear their unique and special children in their own way.

Karen Voke says: *I love my grandchildren to death. It's fun to watch them grow. It's more interesting to sit back and watch the way my girls are raising their children because they are doing things differently than we did.*

Larry Kreider says that he studiously tries to avoid giving his son, Brett, fatherly advice: *I don't want to become a meddling grandfather. Whenever I get a chance, however, I do try to help. For instance, they came over to watch the Super Bowl, and we were having a wonderful time. I mentioned an article that I had read about how important it is to read to the child when he's an infant—children pick up a love of books, and they bond with the parent who is reading to them. I didn't feel as though that was meddling—I was giving Brett some information that I had read.*

Try not to interfere by reprimanding your adult children or giving unwanted advice. Let them parent *their* kids in *their* way.

2. Don't Gloat
In one of his classic comedy routines, Bill Cosby talks about

getting *revenge* on his children by watching them struggle with *their* children. And what parent hasn't said in a moment of frustration, "Just wait till you have children of your own!" There is truth in both of those statements. The only way a person can *truly* understand the frustrations, excitements, agonies, and joys of parenting is to be a parent. Your kids may not understand what you experienced with them until they go through the same situations with their children.

When that happens, you will be tempted to say, "I told you so!" Instead, when your daughter says something like, "I never knew being a mom could be so much work" or your son says, "How did you do it? These kids are driving me crazy," listen, empathize, and offer to help. Your kids don't need to be reminded that they treated you like pond scum—they will feel guilty enough when they begin to receive grief from their own kids.

Karen Voke shares: *The experience of watching my daughters with their children has been a delight. In different ways, each of them has said, "Mom, I had no idea how much you loved me until I held my own." There was no way they could have known. But now, because they've experienced the depth of a parent's love with their own children, there is a different bond between the girls and me.*

3. Don't Spoil

Grandparents are infamous for spoiling their grandchildren. They shower their grandchildren with gifts and let them get away with almost anything. One mother told me that it takes about a week for her to get her daughter back to normal after a trip to her folks. Grandma and Grandpa think she's the "cutest little thing," and they give her whatever she wants. "They'll go into a store and let her pick out a doll or a toy—anything. And then there are all those between-meal snacks of candy and chips!"

Because of your love for your grandchildren, you will be tempted to smother them with gifts and to indulge their bad habits and behavior. But that only causes problems for your children, their parents.

Jerry and Jack Schreur write satirically:

Another good way to antagonize your children is to help them see how much more you love their children than they do. Of course, it might be necessary to spend a little money to bribe your grandchildren with candy, clothes, and toys. Take a few months to prepare for the big moment. Finally it comes. You trot the children into the living room before a large family gathering and ask with a loud voice, "Now, who do you children love best? Mom or Grandma?" Parents are always delighted when their children point to Grandma. (Creative Grandparenting, Grand Rapids: Discovery House, 1992, p. 133.)

That kind of one-upmanship will only hurt your relationship with your kids and, ultimately, with your grandchildren.

This doesn't mean that you can't be generous, but be careful to consult with your child before expressing your generosity.

Also, unless you see signs of child abuse, don't ever circumvent your child's authority or punishment. If they prohibit between-meal treats, don't offer a snack to your grandchild before dinner. If bedtime is 9 P.M., don't keep the grandchild up till 10. If your child doesn't allow the child to watch certain television shows, don't turn them on and say, "What's so bad about this?" And when the grandchild looks to you for support as his mother or father is about to insist on compliance, explain that Mom and Dad are in charge, not you. Support your adult child's efforts to rear their child.

4. Be There

What your children and grandchildren need more than anything else is your availability. If you live nearby, you can be physically present when needed. Your child and their spouse will welcome your presence.

Dottye Luttrell explains: *Grandparenting is so great. Claire knows us and wants to come to us. Being close enough that we can participate is a marvelous blessing. Jennifer and Cliff want us to be part of the baby's life. That makes me think that Jennifer must have good memories and confidence in us—we must have done something right.*

If you live far away and can't be physically present very often, you can still be available by phone. It's good to check in regularly to see how things are going. Keeping the communication lines open gives your child permission to call you with a special request. Make a determined effort to be with your children and grandchildren, even if it is inconvenient and will cost money. They need you.

Be there to advise and guide when necessary and appropriate. Be there to affirm your children as parents and your grandchildren as good, special, and loved. Be there to hug and kiss and play. Karen Voke explains: *Neal can give the grandkids more space. I'm more emotional, more sentimental. The neatest part has been to watch Neal. We would visit Lisa, and I would just want to suffocate Kylie with kisses, but she'd want no part of it. The next thing I knew, however, Grandpa would be in the middle of the floor and had managed to slip her into his lap with his arms around her without her even knowing it.*

We recognize our sacred privilege of praying for our grandchildren. My grandchildren left two little metal cars—one black and one lavender—at our house. I put those cars on my kitchen windowsill as a visible reminder to pray for Jimmy and Lindsay each day.

Joan Biastock

You can also be there to model godliness. I have wonderful scenes etched into my memory of my Grandma Boe studying her Bible. Without knowing it, she had given me a living example of a dedicated Christian and of the importance of God's Word. On a visit to Louisiana to see us, my parents and I sang together in church. Even a year or two later, people would tell me how inspiring it was to see father, mother, and son singing together. My parents were commit-

ted to Christ and to the church, and my daughters knew it.
I also have heard stories from men and women who were
impressed with their grandparents' prayers—their grandparents seemed so close to God. If you have a strong relationship to God, it will shine through your life. Your
grandchildren need a model of what it means to follow
Christ for a lifetime.

Be there for your kids and grandkids—to counsel, play,
hug, pray, laugh, teach, help out, and be an example of one
who truly knows the Lord.

Seeing your children have children is a wonderful privilege—to know that your family's heritage will continue and
that your parenting has come full circle. And there's nothing
quite like the joys of grandparenting. As someone has said,
"You can hold the kids and play with them, but their parents
have to do the dirty work." During this passage, be the kind
of grandparent who is building the next generation for a
lifetime of following Christ.

LET'S THINK ABOUT IT

Warnings

- *Don't expect your kids to rear their children the way you
  reared yours.* They will find their own parenting style.
- *Don't act smug when your kids struggle through the parenting passages as you did.* Pray for them and let them
  discover for themselves what you went through with
  them.
- *Don't spoil your grandchildren with permissiveness and*

excessive gifts. Support your kids in their efforts to be good parents.

Opportunities

- *Give advice and guidance to your kids when asked.* You have a wealth of experience and training from which to draw.
- *Be a cheerleader for your kids and grandkids.* Look for ways to affirm them.
- *Be a good example of a committed follower of Christ.* Show what mature faith looks like.
- *Invest time in your grandchildren.* They need their grandparents.

This is the best season of life! Hallelujah!

Joan and Bob Biastock

Lessons

- *Life is short.* We should make every moment count with our children and grandchildren.
- *Children will not understand what it means to be a parent until they have children of their own.*
- *Grandparents are the link to the past; grandchildren are the link to the future.* We should keep the connection.

Resources

- Jay Kesler, *Grandparenting: The Agony & The Ecstasy*

(Ann Arbor, Mich.: Servant, 1993). Jay draws on his years of experience as president of Youth for Christ/USA, as president of Taylor University, and as a grandparent to give us invaluable insight into grandparenting. The main emphases are sharing spiritual values, building relationships across the miles, providing emotional support if parents divorce, and knowing how and when to intervene in a crisis.

◆ Jerry Schreur and Jack Schreur, *Creative Grandparenting* (Grand Rapids: Discovery House, 1992). This interesting and well-written book is packed with practical help on "how to love and nurture a new generation."

The Pain
and the
Privilege

———

12

I*f* everyone's here, let's begin." The conversations trailed off and the metal chair legs scraped linoleum as the group formed a circle. The leader continued. "We've spent the last few weeks getting to know and trust each other. Now, who has something to share with the group?"

A petite, well-dressed woman was the first to speak. "John couldn't come tonight—he had to work—but we couldn't wait to tell you. . . . We just got the news—I'm pregnant!"

The other group members smiled and voiced their heartfelt congratulations. "That seems so long ago for us, but just like yesterday, too," said a sixtyish man on the other side of the circle. "With our kids now grown and on their own, we wonder where the time went. And speaking of how time flies, I couldn't believe the latest pictures of our grandkids. Our little Emily is going to be a heartbreaker, I tell you." He pulled a black wallet out of his pants pocket and passed it around the circle.

"Let me tell you how I'm feeling," the young man sitting two chairs to the right stated matter-of-factly, but with a frown. "Tired—dog tired! We're up half the night, every night! Plus, we're broke! It costs a lot for baby-sitters these days, not to mention diapers, doctor's visits—"

"Now, Ted, it's not that bad," interrupted his wife, a pleasant-looking woman on his right. "Jeanine is so cute, and she's changing every day. I love being a mother."

"Well, honey, wait till your kid's a teenager like mine," responded a woman on the left. "Taryn's a good kid, but she drives us up the wall with her arguing. We had a fight just before we left, and we had to ground her for a week."

A man next to her took up the conversation. "I'm feeling pretty good, myself. Marcus, our one year old, took his first steps yesterday. I'm going to buy him a basketball and teach him how to dribble. He'll be the next Michael Jordan for sure!"

"That's what I thought when my boy was that age,"

interjected another dad. "But he has found other interests in middle school. At first I was disappointed that he didn't want to go out for the team, but now I'm proud of his accomplishments in music."

"Anyone else?" asked the leader.

After a few seconds of silence, a woman across the circle raised her hand. "Go ahead, Sue," said the leader.

"I don't know how to say this," she began slowly, deliberately, "but I feel so sad . . . and confused. I guess I'm confused about feeling sad, if that makes any sense. Frank and I just dropped Cheri off at college, and I can't seem to stop crying. The house is so quiet and lonely without her. Do you know what I mean?" Dabbing her eyes with a tissue, she dropped her head as Frank put his arm around her and pulled her close.

Gather a cross section of parents in a room and you might find a similar discussion, with just about every emotion expressed, depending on each individual's present experience in the passages of parenting.

In this book we have discussed the possible ups and downs, joys and sorrows, stresses and strains, and pleasures and pains of each of the parenting passages. I have tried to describe *typical* children and *typical* family situations, realizing that a typical family probably doesn't exist. Instead, each family has an endless variety of atypical characteristics, exceptions to the rule. No two families are exactly alike, and neither are the experiences of any two parents—even husband and wife.

Yet we do have so much in common—as children, parents, and grandparents—that we can empathize, laugh, and cry together. Parenting is an adventure, and in our own way and at our own pace, each of us has blazed the same trail.

PAIN

There is one passage that we haven't yet covered. It doesn't fall neatly into chronological order as the others have, but may come to parents at any time. This passage involves pain—deep, severe, gut-wrenching pain. We have already seen that pain is the rule, not the exception to life, and we've discussed the pain of infertility, miscarriage, rebellion, strained relationships, distance, and loneliness. Other painful situations include a teen's struggles with alcohol or drugs and a grown child's troubled marriage or divorce. Pain is woven throughout the parenting experience because we love our kids. We hurt when they hurt from sickness or injury, when they talk back and disobey, when they make poor decisions, and when they leave us. The cliché "love hurts" is profoundly true. Good parents love their children deeply, with no strings attached. Thus, these mothers and fathers will experience pain in the process of parenting.

Kirby Hanawalt tells of a difficult experience: *We were setting up camp in a beautiful area on a lake in the interior of British Columbia. No one was around for miles. Erynn was playing, Sandy was trying to set up our clothesline, I was just finishing setting up our tent, and Ryan was chopping wood for kindling.*

The serene setting was shattered minutes later when Ryan

quietly said, "I cut off my thumb." He had severed the top third of his left thumb with a hatchet. We rushed him to a hospital, about sixty miles away. Four hours and many anxious moments later, the doctor reattached Ryan's thumb with eighteen stitches.

As we waited for God's healing touch to work in Ryan's thumb, we were struck by how quickly life changes. One moment we were all laughing and having a great time camping; the next moment we were anxiously hoping and praying that Ryan would not lose his thumb.

So many times I wanted to take this awful experience from my child. Yet God has drawn Ryan and me closer through this painful moment.

Although each difficult experience brings its own heart-ache, a parent's greatest pain occurs when a child dies. Nothing hurts more than losing a loved one, especially a child. Yet that's the risk we take when we conceive and bring a baby into the world.

For nine months, Jim and Polly McCauley and their two-year-old son, Matt, anxiously awaited the arrival of their new family member. But within a few hours after his birth, the doctors discovered that little Daniel had multiple heart defects and would need surgery within five days. That initial surgery went well, but Jim and Polly knew that eventually their baby would need four or five more operations to correct the problems.

For a year, Daniel grew and developed as a normal child. His vocabulary included *uh-oh, truck,* and *ball,* and he would laugh at Matt's antics at the dinner table. Then, at fifteen months, the time came for the second operation. The surgery went well and the initial prognosis was good. But forty-eight hours later, he began to decline rapidly. Then he was gone. Daniel McCauley had died.

Polly explains: *When we first heard about the heart defects, we were shocked and disbelieving. Then we prayed, realizing that we didn't have control.*

I was much less prepared for Daniel's death than Jim. We knew Daniel was different for a reason, and I really believed he would make it—that it was God's purpose to heal him. I guess I thought I had God's plan all figured out. But the ground dropped out from under me when Daniel died.

Jim and I dealt with our grief in different ways. I cried a lot, and Jim worked out his feelings by renovating the basement. We were aware of the statistics about marriages falling apart in situations like ours, so we had some counseling. And we tried not to judge each other for how we were dealing with our sorrow. I turned back to the Lord—to the God who loves me. One thing that helped a lot in my grief was reading about others who also had experienced the loss of a child, others who had suffered the same pain. Journaling also was a great help—I was able to pour out my feelings on paper. Today those journal pages are invaluable to me because I can read how I felt at the time—I don't want to forget my son.

After the first year, the grief was still very real. And now, even though five years have passed, sorrow still sweeps over me at times, especially in church when we're singing about heaven. Often I just want Daniel back, and I wonder what he would be like at this age.

Shortly after Daniel's death, God blessed us with another

pregnancy, and he gave us a little girl, Kelsey—I think another boy right away would have been tough to handle. But recently I gave birth to a son, Christopher.

God taught me much through this experience, but two lessons stand out. First, I can't see how people can possibly endure the severe illness or death of a child without God and the hope of heaven. Second, I am much more aware of what a gift children are and that they aren't really ours—they're God's.

Jim also shares his perspective on the loss of their son: *Thinking that our son would die was beyond our comprehension. We knew we had a special little baby who needed special care. We thought that caring for Daniel would be our privilege and our challenge. We never dreamed that we would have Daniel for just a little while.*

Concerning how we dealt with our grief, we had to realize that God made us different. Polly's more emotional, and I'm more verbal. I needed to talk it out, but it was too difficult for Polly to talk about. We both had to learn not to judge each other and to accept and listen to each other.

The biggest lesson I learned through this experience is the whole issue of control. We Americans have a compulsion to think that we have everything organized and protected—that we are in control. But control is a fantasy. I felt totally helpless when Daniel had his operation. It was like the doctors were saying to us, "You sit out here; we're going to take your baby. . . ." And of course the ultimate loss of control was when Daniel died. Through this I learned that I shouldn't worry about control but about obedience and submission . . . to the Lord.

There is no way to minimize the pain of parents when they lose a child. Their suffering runs deep; their grief may last for years. John White offers this advice to parents in pain:

> *Do not grieve alone. There must be someone, somewhere with whom you can share your pain. Find that someone. I know that you may have shared your pain with God. However, I speak of a fellow human. I agree that not everyone will want to share your burden. You may question your right to share it. Yet Christian fellowship exists, among other things, for the sharing of pain and of pleasure. Pain shared is pain divided. Pleasure shared is pleasure multiplied. Therefore Christian fellowship, where it is a true sharing-praying fellowship, can be a resource of incalculable value. (Parents in Pain, Downers Grove, Ill.: InterVarsity Press, 1979, pp. 243–244)*

Parenting can be difficult and painful, but through the pain and sorrow, we can have hope and joy. For one day:

> *All the Christians who have died will suddenly become alive, with new bodies that will never, never die; and then we who are still alive shall suddenly have new bodies, too. For our earthly bodies, the ones we have now that can die, must be transformed into heavenly bodies that cannot perish but will live forever. When this happens, then at last this Scripture will come true—"Death is swallowed up in victory." O death, where then your victory? Where then*

*your sting? For sin—the sting that causes death—will all
be gone; and the law, which reveals our sins, will no longer
be our judge. How we thank God for all of this! It is he
who makes us victorious through Jesus Christ our Lord!
(1 Corinthians 15:52-57, TLB)*

Thank God for his promise of eternal life and that in
heaven, "He will wipe away all tears from their eyes, and
there shall be no more death, nor sorrow, nor crying, nor
pain. All of that has gone forever" (Revelation 21:4, TLB).

In heaven we will be reunited with our boys and girls who
have died. Children who have been distant will be close.
And those who are handicapped will be whole.

PRIVILEGE

Psalm 127:3-5 states: "Sons are a heritage from the Lord,
children a reward from him. Like arrows in the hands of a
warrior are sons born in one's youth. Blessed is the man
whose quiver is full of them" (NIV).

Whether our children were planned or surprises, whether
they joined our family through birth or adoption, being a
parent is an honor. God has given us the distinct privilege
and responsibility of caring for his little ones. We are to
welcome and care for them (Matthew 18:1-6; Mark 9:36-
37), teach them (Deuteronomy 6:7), discipline and train
them (Proverbs 13:24; 22:6; Ephesians 6:4), pray for them
(Job 1:5), love them (1 Corinthians 13; Titus 2:4; 1 John
4:7-12), and enjoy them (Psalm 113:9; Proverbs 5:18;
17:6).

Bob Stromberg explains: *When Judy and I first got married,* **many** *people said to us, "Well, enjoy it now, 'cause when the kids come, everything'll change." Of course it did, but what bothered me was the tone of voice that these people used. They made it sound like things would not be as good when the kids came.*

After the kids arrived, these same people said, "Well, enjoy it when they're babies, 'cause when they start crawling around, it gets a lot tougher." Same tone of voice. And they continued through the years. "Sure it's fun now, but wait until the terrible twos; wait until they leave you and go off to school; wait until junior high school; wait until they're driving; wait until they head off to college; wait until your youngest leaves for good; wait until you two are all alone." Always the same foreboding tone.

Judy and I are now through over half of these passages, and I can honestly say we've enjoyed each more than the last. Right now, I dread the thought of our children leaving and being off on their own, but I know from experience that, when the time comes, it will be time. It will be right. That doesn't mean I didn't weep when my eldest grabbed his lunch bucket and headed for kindergarten, but it means I wouldn't have wanted it any other way.

Judy and I never have—nor will we ever—go toward any of our passages with a "just wait until" negative attitude. I think people who do so soon find that their lives are over and they missed them.

Parenting is not always rosy, not always easy, and not always rewarding. In fact, as we have seen, it may contain a lot of tough times and heartache. But it is God's will.

Regardless of our situation and our kids' temperaments, personalities, abilities, and limitations, our goal should be to do our best so that we may hear God's affirmation: "Well done, good and faithful servant!" (Matthew 25:21, NIV).

In a poignant moment, Neil Wilson received one of the rewards of parenting: *When Nathan was about six, he happened to be present one evening when I was speaking at a dinner for the local Awana group. I was telling a rather emotional story and got caught up in my feelings. I paused for a moment to collect myself, but almost completely lost control in what happened next. I suddenly realized that Nathan had left his seat and had come to stand beside me. His little arm reached as high as he could around my waist, and we stood facing the audience together. He couldn't have said it better: My dad will be all right in a minute if you just bear with him.*

Where are you in this series of parenting passages? Enjoy it. Make the most of it. Cherish each moment with your children and your grandchildren. Prepare them for the future by bringing them up "in the training and instruction of the Lord" (Ephesians 6:4, NIV). And release them to God's loving care.

Additional titles from Dave Veerman

Parenting Passages is also available on Tyndale Living Audio.
0-8423-7432-9

FROM DAD WITH LOVE
With Chuck Aycock   0-8423-1333-8
Raise confident kids by giving them priceless, character-building gifts.

GETTING YOUR HUSBAND TO TALK
With Gail Veerman   0-8423-1325-7
100+ ideas to get conversations going with your husband.

GETTING YOUR KID TO TALK
0-8423-1326-5
100+ ideas to get conversations going with your children.

HOW TO APPLY THE BIBLE
0-8423-1384-2
Proven techniques for applying God's Word—based on the *Life Application Bible*.

THE ONE YEAR BIBLE MEMORY BOOK FOR FAMILIES
0-8423-1387-7
Daily verses, review questions, and notes help families memorize and understand Scripture.